For All That I Found There

Caroline Blackwood

Duckworth

First published in 1973 by
Gerald Duckworth & Co Ltd
The Old Piano Factory
43 Gloucester Crescent, London NW1

© Caroline Blackwood 1973

Acknowledgments are due to the editors of periodicals in which
some of the pieces in this book first appeared, as follows : to the
London Magazine for *Please Baby Don't Cry, Who Needs It?, The Baby
Nurse, The Interview* and *How You Love Our Lady*; to the *Listener*
for *Women's Theatre* and *Memories of Ulster*; to *Encounter* for
Portrait of the Beatnik.

Printed in Great Britain by
Bristol Typesetting Company Limited
Barton Manor, St Philips, Bristol

For All That I Found There

CONTENTS

FOR CAL

Fiction

PLEASE BABY DON'T CRY

The old woman usually stayed in her room. Now that his wife was in hospital she was frisking round his kitchen in a frilly nylon wrap and her hair was done up in curlers. Lou Alton noticed that his mother-in-law's wizened little face looked animated, rested, almost rosy. She seemed rejuvenated by her daughter's operation.

'Do you think she should have done it, Lou?' she asked him.

'I wouldn't know.'

'I guess it must be all over. They were going to do it early.'

'I guess so.' The old woman was right. It must be all over. The surgeons must have already finished their stitch-work on the sagging skin of those large bitter eyes.

'You know I just can't wait to see her,' his mother-in-law said.

'I just bet you can't.'

'I don't imagine that she will let me go to visit her in the hospital.' The old woman's voice sounded suddenly plaintive. 'She's always acted mean with me. It's funny, you know, Lou. Cyd and I have always been very close—but we have never really got on. I guess you may have noticed it.'

He had most certainly noticed it. He had been extremely surprised three months ago when his wife suddenly told him that she had arranged for her mother to live with them. 'But you have always told me that you couldn't stand her!' 'What do you want me to do with her, for Christ's sake?' Cyd had shouted. 'Shove her down the garbage-disposal?' He found out later that his mother-in-law had just been fired from her job in one of the Hollywood film studios where she had worked for some years as a telephone operator. She had been caught selling indiscreet items to the fan magazines. She gathered her information by listening in to the private telephone conversations of the Stars.

'She's house-trained,' his wife had said to him. 'She won't be any bother.' The old woman had certainly been very little bother. She very rarely came

9

out of her room. She shuffled out occasionally and made herself a furtive piece of toast in the kitchen. Then she shuffled discreetly back and shut the door.

'What on earth does she do with herself shut up in that room all day?' he often asked Cyd.

'What the Hell do you care? She's not bothering you.' He had still been bothered by her silence, by the faint little scuffling sounds that he heard some-times in the night. His mother-in-law reminded him of some sick old animal crouching alone behind her shut door.

'She would be better off in a dog's home,' he told Cyd. 'Why don't you ever speak one word to her? You could ask her to join us sometimes for a drink, or even a meal. It certainly wouldn't kill you.'

'You can speak to her if you are so crazy about her,' she always answered. 'Have all your meals with the old cunt. I'm not stopping you.'

The old woman had developed an abscess. She crept silently round the house for a couple of days with her swollen face wrapped up in a tea-cloth. Finally Cyd drove her into Beverly Hills to get her tooth pulled. He had sud-denly gone into the old woman's room. It smelled so stale and perfumed. She hadn't opened her windows since she had arrived. He had gone through all her drawers. He had felt like a sleep-walker. He was looking for something. It was important. He had no idea why. He would only know what it was when he found it. Among her musty stays and night-dresses he had found a large pile of papers. He had picked out a page. The hand-writing was the thin scratch of a ball-point. 'THE LAST WILL AND TESTAMENT OF ALICE ROSE MARTINI. To my daughter Cyd. Now that I am dead, Cyd, I feel I can say so much to you. I have wanted to say so much for so long but I knew you would not want to listen. I hate leaving you knowing that everything is going so bad for you. I never thought that Lou was right. You used to have so much to offer. As a girl you had looks, you had so much personality. You could have really gone anywhere. You could have made it really big in movies. I don't listen, but I can't help hearing when the house is quiet at night. And then after all these years seeing you still with no kids. I just can't help putting two and two together. He's not really a man. I knew it the moment I first set eyes on him. And you deserve a real man if anyone does. Anyway—everything I have I leave to you. I don't have much as you know. Life was pretty tough on me and your father acted like a louse. I have always had to work all my life. I wanted you to have nice things—Education—all the things I never had. Now when I see the life you lead with Lou I wonder if it was all worth it. Anyway, I leave you the tortoise-shell combs that belonged to Mother. I leave you the brown chair, the one that I brought with me, the one that you now have in your living-room. I notice that you behave as if it was yours already. You never even seem to try to stop Lou putting up his feet on it. The cushions are getting really ruined. I haven't said anything. But I can't help minding rather. Anyway, now that it is really yours at last maybe you will take more care with it . . .'

He had found many other drafts. 'Dear Cyd . . .' The old spider sitting in her room spinning her wills. 'He's not really a man.' And her daughter most certainly was not really a woman – that was weak – it merely showed she had known where to hit him. He had never mentioned the wills to Cyd. He wondered sometimes what she would think of them. She would certainly not want to let him know. She would shrug of course, smile sarcastically with one eyebrow raised. 'So what about them for Christ's sake? Do they really bother you?'

'Can I fix you a nice little breakfast, Lou?' his mother-in-law was now asking him. She had become so bold now that her daughter was in hospital. She was not making herself any more dry little pieces of toast. She was frying herself eggs, and bacon, and sausages. She was bending over the pan and inhaling the fumes of the fat. She was squeezing herself fresh orange juice, smearing great dollops of jam on her cereal. She was even making herself waffles with a waffle-iron. Did he really need Cyd? Alice Rose Martini must surely be asking herself the same question. Would the two of them really be happier just making a life of it together? The old woman could go on making her wills. He could go on going to the office. Meals would certainly be very much better. Cyd resented even opening a can. Alice Rose Martini really had a far more cheerful disposition than her daughter. At least she seemed to be really enjoying her waffle. She was making designs on it with syrup, golden spirals, great ornate curlicues. Cyd just sat all day on the Swedish sofa, smoking and drinking her Martinis. She crossed and uncrossed her long thin legs and stared through the plate-glass windows down to the sea.

'You know something, Lou?' The old woman's mouth was crusted golden with waffle-syrup. 'I didn't sleep one wink last night for worrying. I never liked to say a word to Cyd, but I really don't quite trust her doctor.'

'She found him,' he said.

'I never liked to say a word to you, Lou. But I just kept hoping that you would make her go to one of the really top-flight Beverly Hills guys. One of the ones that do the big Stars.'

'I hardly knew a thing about it. She arranged the whole thing herself. Dot Mansville and the rest of the girls put her up to it. I always thought the whole idea was quite sick, completely crazy. All I wanted was for her to leave me out of it. I figured that it was her operation.'

'She would have gone to a decent doctor if you had made her.' Behind her rhinestone-encrusted spectacles the old woman's eyes glittered accusingly. 'Who's going to pay for it all for Christ's sake? She would have had to listen to you, Lou, and you know it. You are so goddam scared of her, Lou. That's always been your trouble. If anything goes wrong I swear I'll always blame you. You could have told her that it was your operation.'

'I just didn't see it like that,' he said. He should have seen it like that. The old buzzard was quite right. In a sense it really was his own operation. Its object, he could only assume, was the removal of himself. Before his wife could free herself from him, she had first felt bound to free herself from all the excess fatty eye-tissue which she felt tied her to him. The concept had a certain primitive grandeur. The sacrifice of the part, for the salvation of the whole.

'I guess you will be going to visit her in hospital,' Alice Rose Martini said to him.

'I guess so.' The idea had not even occurred to him. He rang his office. 'I won't be in today. My wife has been taken to hospital.'

'One thing I'll say for you, Lou,' the old woman said, sitting down in the breakfast alcove with all her waffles and her sausages, 'you work hard and you've given her a lovely home.'

'I guess it's O.K.' He looked round the living-room. It had a sofa, two steel chairs and a lamp. It had a pile of magazines on a table. It looked as impersonal, sterile, and neat, as any hospital waiting-room. It was certainly O.K. It was probably as good a place as any, if you had to wait somewhere for fifteen years to have your operation.

'Why don't you give yourself a break, Lou?' the old woman asked him. 'Why don't we both take it easy and maybe go down to the beach?'

'I prefer to stay here in the house,' he said. He had never very much liked the beach. He had always been depressed by the flat enervated waters of the Pacific. He had very little desire to sit with his mother-in-law on the grubby sands where the homosexual muscle-boys played their perpetual ball and the bums from Santa Monica lay choking in the sun.

'What will you do with yourself here all day?' the old woman asked him.

'Hang around.' He felt suddenly restless and irritable. It seemed to him now that his wife, by her one decisive attempt to defy and reverse her destiny, had totally succeeded in defying and reversing the roles of their relationship. She had finally found, in the inaction of the anaesthetised, the needed action which had always eluded her in their marriage. She was now free-wheeling on a hospital trolley up the corridors of a future. Now he was on the Swedish sofa, static and disgruntled with nothing to do but wait.

'Cyd's got guts,' her mother said to him. 'She's certainly got guts, whatever else you like say about her. I guess she's given you a pretty rough time of it, Lou. It's sometimes hard to know what's really eating her. I guess she's never really known what she wanted. I always hoped that you would make her try to get into movies. When you married her I really hoped that you would help her find herself.'

The telephone rang. It was the doctor.

'How did it go?'

'I am afraid I can't possibly tell you that until her eye bandages come off. We will know how it went when we have been able to take a thorough look at the healing.' The doctor sounded brisk and bored.

'When will they come off?'

'That, I'm afraid, I can't begin to tell you, Mr Alton. No case is ever the same. It all really depends on the healing.'

'But I don't quite understand how you can tell how the healing is unless you first take the bandages off to see.' He knew he sounded ridiculous, medically a moron. But he suddenly felt that these fatuous and persistent inquiries about her bandages were the very last gesture he would ever be prepared to make to his wife.

'When your wife's bandages are ready to come off, Mr Alton, I will certainly let you know.' The doctor was becoming increasingly impatient. He clearly wanted to ring off before his professional secrets could be any further threatened by the idiot curiosity of the amateur.

'When will Mrs Alton be able to see me?' He hoped that in one incisive, surgical sentence, the doctor would tell him that it would be for ever impossible. He had not the slightest desire to see Cyd with her new eyes – eyes that had been both created and bandaged by this most disagreeable brisk voice on the telephone.

'Naturally,' the doctor said in the slow and heavily patient tones sometimes employed to children and the feeble-minded, 'Mrs Alton will only be able to see you after her eye-bandages have been taken off.' He laughed, a dry little sarcastic puff of a laugh. 'You can really hardly expect her to see you, or anyone else, while she has still got them on!'

'Are you pleased with the results of the operation, Doctor?'

'Mr Alton, I think I have already told you that I am not prepared to give any opinion until I have taken a proper look at the healing.'

After the doctor had rung off Lou Alton rang his wife at the hospital.

'Are you O.K.?'

'Sure I'm O.K. I'm fine. I'm really great. I can't speak to you though, I am not meant to take calls today.' Her voice sounded muffled and remote, as though she were speaking through a diver's tube from the bottom of the sea. It sounded oddly sensuous, friendly and pleased. He realised then that she was still half-anaesthetised.

'Shall I come to see you tomorrow?'

She grunted, purred. His words had no meaning to her. He repeated them, shouting with the frantic, unreasonable anger with which he sometimes found himself addressing the deaf.

'No, no,' she whispered happily. 'There's no point in your coming to see me.' Her voice trailed away. 'I'm absolutely fine . . .'

The next day Lou Alton drove down town to see his wife in the hospital. A bunch of kids were demonstrating, they had tied up the traffic all the way along the Strip. He found it intolerably hot and aggravating to sit waiting for the cops to disperse them, while his car radio crackled out love tunes and his eyes streamed from the exhaust fumes of the great snakes of stationary cars. For the love of Christ, what did they think they were demonstrating? If they were against the War he was certainly with them. And he would be far more with them if they would only let the traffic move. Maybe they only wanted legalised pot. How the hell could you tell from their placards? 'Love!' 'Love!' 'Politicians take a trip!' How could they expect anyone who was sane to join them for Love? He disliked seeing them smashed with the night-sticks. But why must the silly little pricks paint their faces with blue zodiac signs? Why must they have beads and dirty feet? Cyd had always said he was a fascist. Cyd had said he was so many things. But surely these kids themselves when they were older would not very much care to be forced to sit in the steaming Hell of a traffic snarled to a standstill, nor would they wish to have 'Love!' and 'Take a Trip' signs waved and cracked against their car windows – not if the only trip they were trying to make was to a Downtown Los Angeles hospital – not if they were trying to visit a wife who had just completed her facial operation.

'Are you an expectant?' a nurse was asking him. He was finally in the lobby of the hospital, an ugly orange building that squatted among dusty and distressed-looking palm-trees in the suffocating smog-hazed sun. 'You don't want

Maternity. You want Vanity.' He followed the nurse down long bleak anti-septic corridors. 'Vanity' seemed to be thriving. It had all the bustle and activity of a prosperous factory. Muzac blared from the ceiling. Women kept passing him; some were being wheeled, some were hobbling. He saw faces patched purple with iodine, tufted with great beards of discoloured cotton-wool, faces that were a fence-work of surgical tape. He saw women with plasters covering their entire neck and shoulders. They were White Knights – they were Martians. Their only eyes were the great black holes that had been cut in their plasters.

'What's that?' he asked the nurse. He could hear screaming. 'That's a face-peeling job.'

'Why the Christ don't they give her an anaesthetic?'

'They did when it was done.'

'Then why on earth is she still screaming?'

'You'd be screaming if you had what she's got. They have to burn so deep, you see, and they have to cover such very large areas. The problem is that you can't really keep a patient under all the time it takes for the raw under-skin to toughen. The technique was started in the war you know, they got the idea from working with burnt pilots. We used to give the face-peelings morphine but it led to addiction and complications. We've had them die on us from shock, you know. The hospital isn't responsible. The old fools do it at their own risk. They want to have skin like a baby and so they keep on coming.'

His wife was lying completely motionless when he came in to her grim and strongly disinfected ward. He was shocked by the change in her appear-ance. Her whole body seemed to have shrunk since her operation and her skin had the ashen and papery fragility of someone very old. One of her eyes was still bandaged, which gave her face the unsuitably jaunty air of a pirate. Her other socket was so hideously swollen and disfigured that he found it almost impossible to believe that it still contained an eye at all. The surgeon's knife had cut a neat circle from under the line of her eyelashes to the arch of her eyebrows. The wound still looked fresh and bloody and against its cheerful redness huge casual stitches stood out like the legs of a giant beetle. He stood awkwardly in the middle of her ward. He could think of nothing to say.

'I expect it looks kind of awful. I haven't had the guts to look at it.' Her voice was flat and low. She seemed so drained, so dispirited.

'It looks fine.' She lay back on her pillows without answering. A shaft of

15

morning sun trickled through the window of her ward and made patterns on her bed.

'I think that they have cut off all my bottom eye-lashes.' She was whining suddenly with the plaintive petulance of a child. 'Can you see if any of them are left?' Her eyelashes had been long and silky. In her present state of physical exhaustion their loss seemed the only thing which could arouse her to any great degree of concern. He looked at the pulp of livid flesh under her eye. He looked at its thick black network of stitches.

'It's rather difficult to see.' He saw her whole body twitch with nervous anger as though his inability to see any trace of her eyelashes in some way typified an ineffectuality that she had resented for so long.

'I'm expecting Dot Mansville in a little while.' Her voice had regained its old aggressive crackle. 'They don't like me to have more than one visitor at a time.'

'Do you want me to go, then?'

'No, it's not that. It's just that I don't see much point in your staying here hanging around.'

The next day he again visited her in the hospital. His wife was still bandaged and he sensed a very great hostility emanating from the slit in the swelling which was still all that could be seen of her free eye.

'Dot Mansville and some of the girls came here yesterday,' she said provocatively. 'They all think I'm going to be much better once it's healed.'

'Better for whom? Better for what?' He regretted his words immediately, for although he could tell that he had succeeded in wounding her, his success seemed rather unnecessary, for lying there on her pillows with her purple-jellied eye and her bandages, she looked already so badly wounded as to be almost beyond retrieval. She lay very still. When she finally spoke her voice sounded odd and muffled.

'Please don't try to make me cry, Lou. They say if I cry I'll tear my stitches and get an infection.' He watched, chilled, as a bright drop of crystal water squeezed out of the tiny aperture in the mound of discoloured and inflamed flesh, and slowly trickled down her blue bruised cheek.

'Please don't cry, Baby. I didn't mean to be mean.' Tears immediately started gushing out of her raw pulp of a socket.

'For Christ's sake, stop!' He was shouting. 'What had I better do? For Christ's sake stop, before you tear your stitches and give yourself an infection! I think I'd better get the nurse!'

'How can the nurse stop me crying? How can anyone ever stop me crying

16

now? If I get an infection, I just get an infection. What the Hell does it matter? Why the fucking Hell should I care what happens to me any more?' The disastrous appearance of her face was intensified by her weeping. And yet as he watched her choking on her pillows, so disfigured and distressed, she repulsed him no more than she had in all the years that she had been so well-groomed, composed, and caustic, and sitting complaining on his sofa and drinking her martinis with Dot Mansville and 'the girls'. He saw for a moment in this eye-less, moaning, middle-aged woman some echo of the vulnerability of the nervous girl he had once wanted to protect. He saw also in the fearful distortion of the face he had once loved the squalor of this self-centred and dis-satisfied personality who now through vanity had deprived itself even of eyes with which to cry. On an impulse he went over to her bed and kissed the purple festering slit from which her tears were still attempting to roll. He noticed a sweet-sour taste of disinfectant mingled with blood and salt.

'Don't cry, Baby,' he said mechanically. 'Please, Baby, don't cry.' Baby! He thought. How ludicrous. Some baby.

His gesture seemed to please her. She shivered. She clutched at him grate-fully. She threw her arms round his neck and clung to him like a child.

'How can you bear to kiss it, Lou?' she said. 'I vomit if I even look at it.'

'I'm sorry if I upset you,' he soothed. Instantly her whole body twitched in a fierce spasm of nervous irritation. He had patronised her, disappointed, infuriated her. She wrenched herself violently away from him. 'Oh cut it out for Christ's sake!' she shouted. 'I'm sick to death of those lyrics. Why the Hell should you think that anything you do or say can upset me any more? Don't you see, you fool, that I'm nearly going out of my mind because of the ban-dage.'

'What's wrong with the bandage?'

'Nothing's wrong with the bandage, idiot! But why the fucking Hell haven't they come to take it off?'

'Should they have taken it off?' The idea had never occurred to him. He had taken the bandage's presence for granted as one of the inevitable intricacies of the whole ritualistic operation.

'Of course it should if the other one has!' Her voice rose in a scream. 'Only the bastards obviously don't dare show me what's happened underneath!'

'Have you asked the nurses why it hasn't been taken off?'

'I can't ask them anything, you fool! They are all a bunch of lousy Black Power spades. And Christ if you knew how they hate the Vanity patients! They really despise us. They resent us for taking up their time, which they think

B

should be given to the really sick. They have hardly been near me all day. And when they do come they won't say a word. So I have just been lying here hour after hour, never knowing if I have lost the sight of one eye and all my own fault.'

'I'll call the doctor immediately. And for Christ's sake stop worrying. Your eye is obviously quite all right.' He had no longer any very strong feeling that her eye was obviously quite all right. The bandage looked extremely sinister now that its presence was questioned. He, too, was now convinced that it was concealing some miserable mistake.

'There's something else!' his wife shouted to him as he was leaving her ward. 'You have got to tell that fucking doctor that I will never let him take my stitches out!'

'Honey,' he said. 'You can't keep your stitches in for ever.'

'I don't care, you fool!' she was screaming again. 'You can tell that doctor that I'd far rather die than ever let him take them out! He has already half-blinded me, hasn't he? Isn't that enough? Do you think I care now if I always keep my stitches in? I've been through as much as I can take! Can you imagine what it would be like to have him poking around with his tweezers in the middle of the wounds? It makes me vomit just to think of it. I just can't have any more pain, Lou! Can't you understand that? I just can't take any more! You have got to tell that son of a bitch of a doctor that I will never let him take them out!'

'I will do what I can.' He walked out into the tiled corridor in which, mingling with Muzac, he could still hear the screams of the woman with the face-peeling job. He stopped a nurse who was hurrying past with a plate of red jelly on a tray.

'My wife seems very upset. Can you give her some sedation?'

'Of course she's upset. They are all upset. Who wouldn't be upset in a dump like this? I'm upset too.' She scuttled irritably away.

The doctor sounded cold and impatient when he was finally reached by telephone. 'I'm afraid I haven't had time to get round to your wife today. I've been up to my neck in the theatre. I'll try and drop by tomorrow and take her eye stitches out.'

'She doesn't want them taken out.'

'Well, I'm afraid I really just couldn't care less whether she wants them out or not. If we leave them in much longer we are very likely to find ourselves with a very pretty little infection.'

'I don't think you have quite taken in her state of mind, Doctor. She's really

18

blowing her cool. If she has any more pain at the moment I think she might really flip.'

'There may be discomfort – but there is really very little pain attached to the taking out of stitches.'

'I don't think it's the pain she minds. I think it's more the idea of your touching her wounds.'

'Oh well, really, Mr Alton, I'm afraid that simply can't be helped. Your wife is a grown woman and she will just have to get herself used to the idea pretty quick. Her stitches have quite obviously got to come out and that is that.'

'Could you give her a general anaesthetic when she has her stitches out?'

He heard the doctor gasp. 'A general anaesthetic to have stitches out! Oh yes! That would be quite something! And who do you think is going to find the time to administer it to her? You might remember that your wife is not the only woman in the hospital. Has it occurred to you, Mr Alton, that there might be other patients who might possibly have priority?'

'I will make it worth your while, Doctor. I am quite willing to pay any extra charges.'

The doctor capitulated, grudgingly, as though he were humouring an unfortunate. 'If it's really worth it to you, Mr Alton, if you really want to go in for something so needlessly time-consuming and costly, I suppose I will have to go along with you. It still beats me why your wife can't make do with a local.'

'Would that mean that she would have to have needles stuck into the surrounds of her eyes?'

'Naturally.'

'I insist that you give her a general. And there's just one other thing, Doctor.' The doctor seemed about to ring off. 'Why hasn't her second bandage come off?'

'We were not quite satisfied with the healing.'

'Is that quite customary?'

'Under the circumstances, yes. You know, of course, that we ran into complications.'

'I didn't know. How could I possibly know? What precisely were the complications?'

'Well, to complete a satisfactory drainage of the tissue under her brows, we had to cut away more fatty surplus than is generally our practice. The removal of the excess under the eye itself went more or less as intended.'

'Does that mean that the eye under the bandage has been damaged?'

'No more so than the eye which is at present unbandaged. The sight of both will be completely unaffected if that's what you are getting at. She will, of course, have always just one problem. She will never, of course, quite be able to close her eyes at night.'

'Could you possibly be more explicit, Doctor? What exactly do you mean – never quite close her eyes at night?'

'Exactly what I said. As you know we had to drag all the skin above her eyes upwards, in order to stitch it to the eyebrow line where her scars would not show. And then as I told you she had quite a really astounding amount of excess fatty tissue. We had no choice. We had to cut it away. Naturally we couldn't do this without seriously restricting the mobility of her eye-lids. But there was simply no other way of giving her that really taut and youthful look she wanted. I don't think she should be too bothered by it. In my experience women don't usually care too much about how they look when they are sleeping. Most of them become accustomed to the light after a few months. If they find it a problem they simply wear an eye-mask. There is really one thing that I will have to warn your wife – she may of course have a little trouble with formation.'

'Formation?'

'Naturally the inability to shut her eyes when she sleeps may result in some sort of matinal formation on the over-exposed eye-ball, a congested film of dust, eye-mucous, etc. She will be able to get rid of it, of course, by bathing her eyes very thoroughly every morning with optrex or boracic. I think that in general both yourself and Mrs Alton will be very satisfied with the results of the operation. You will certainly find that she has quite an improved appearance.'

'Is there nothing you can do to make it possible for her to close her eyes at night, Doctor?'

'Nothing I am afraid, Mr Alton. When you are dealing with something as delicate as eye-tissue, you can't really replace what is cut away.'

Lou Alton started walking slowly back to his wife's ward. He turned suddenly and went back to the hospital lobby. He wanted to talk to someone. A nurse. Anyone. Another Vanity patient. He went to a telephone and rang his wife's mother.

'How is she?' He heard the greedy throb of the old woman's excitement. He thought of waffle-syrup.

'She's fine.'

'How does she look?'

'Oh, she really looks magnificent.'

'Oh gee! Isn't that terrific! I bet she looks just gorgeous! I bet she's never looked cuter. I just can't wait to see her.'

'She's never looked better. She's probably never had more to offer.'

'Well, isn't that quite something? The things they can do nowadays. It's really just fantastic. I guess she should have had it done much sooner.'

'Maybe she should have had it done at birth,' he said. 'These things are so very hard to say.'

'Some of them have started quite late, you know,' the old woman said.

'Some of what have started late?' His mind was working slowly.

'The Big Names, of course,' she said impatiently. 'Some of the really Top Flight Stars.'

'I guess they have. I have never really thought about that.'

'I guess that you had better look out now, Lou!' The old woman's voice sounded suddenly waggish. 'You have had her to yourself for quite a long time, you know.'

'I most certainly have.' A stream of images flashed through his brain like the ugly rising past of a drowning man.

'Well, I must say you don't sound too overjoyed, Lou. Maybe you never really wanted her operation to work out too well. Maybe you thought that you were sitting pretty. Maybe you just wanted for things to go on staying that way.'

'Maybe.' He was wondering what he would tell his wife when he next saw her. He decided that he would tell her that the sight of her bandaged eye was completely unaffected, that she would be totally unconscious during the removal of her stitches. How was he to tell her that her eyes would never again close – that in the nights they would stare forever into the darkness as though they searched even in sleep for the solution that had always eluded them in waking?

WHO NEEDS IT?

'Saturdays are crazy! Saturdays kill me!' Angeline said to Mrs Reilly.

'Saturdays are a problem for everyone.' Mrs Reilly stared mournfully at her own reflection in Angeline's mirror.

'Every week it's always the same story.' Angeline carefully formed a kiss-curl on Mrs Reilly's wrinkled forehead. 'Saturdays all the girls come in at once – "Can you touch up my roots, Angeline?" – "Angeline, I'm going out tonight and I look as brassy as the morning sun. Can you give me a bit of a tone down?" You know how it is, Mrs Reilly. The girls would all rather be seen walking naked down Broadway, than be seen weekends without their hair fixed. I just hate to disappoint a customer – but if you've only got two hands, what are you going to do?'

'Nothing else to do,' Mrs Reilly sighed.

'Saturdays are just so crazy, Mrs Reilly! Half the week I'm sitting here all alone in the shop with only my own hair dryers for company. So I give myself a bleach or sometimes a set of highlights – and then I give myself another bleach and a different set of highlights. My husband says he likes a change. I guess that husbands do like changes really. All the same it's a very good way to ruin your hair messing around with it all day long like that – but if your shop's dead empty what else are you going to do?'

'Nothing else to do,' Mrs Reilly sighed again.

'My husband always knows when business has been lousy when he sees me coming home with a brand new hair colour.'

'They always know.' Mrs Reilly stared gloomily at Angeline's floor, which was littered with hair clippings, pins, rollers, and cigarette butts, and stained with great patches of old purple dye.

'My husband's never stopped telling me that I've got to do something about Saturdays, Mrs Reilly. "Look," he says "you want *Angeline's Beauty Salon* to be a friendly kind of a place – informal – somewhere where the girls can all drop in without an appointment and have themselves a ball – a place where it's a real pleasure to go. Now once you start turning away customers on Saturdays, Angeline – you can really be in trouble. I mean that's no pleasure for them".'

'No pleasure in that, Angeline.' Mrs Reilly shook her head. 'Your husband's quite right.'

Angeline handed Mrs Reilly a hand-mirror. 'How do you like the back flipping out like that? I think it's just darling – so much younger. Anyway, Mrs Reilly, I figured I really better do something about weekends. So now you see that woman over there – that's Mrs Klein. I've got her to come in Saturdays to give me a hand with the rinses. She used to work in the Beauty business before the war. It's hard nowadays to get people who know the work.'

'Nowadays,' Mrs Reilly fidgeted irritably with her own grey curls, 'people won't work.'

'It's like a favour for Mrs Klein. She needs the extra, you know how it is.' Angeline bent over and whispered in Mrs Reilly's ear. 'She's Jewish you know. She was in one of those camps in Europe. Very tragic.'

Mrs Reilly turned and stared at Mrs Klein who was down at the other end of the Beauty Salon rubbing a froth of henna dye into the unsuitably long, mermaid-like hair of an elderly woman with spectacles.

'You'd never know it.' Mrs Reilly gave another of her heavy sighs.

'Well, I just wouldn't like to say that. Mrs Klein is not as old as she looks, you know. You see the big black circles under her eyes. It's aged her. No question about that. I want you to have spray today, Mrs Reilly. It's windy outside and it will help to hold your set.'

It was getting very hot in Angeline's sleazy Beauty Salon. Her hair dryers hummed monotonously as they puffed out their dry, burnt air. Women were sitting under them in rows like bored warriors wearing chipped steel helmets. The cheap strip-lighting threw a sickly, green light on to Angeline's dirty basins and her piles of battered *Vogues*.

Miss Ferguson, an earnest little weasel-faced stenographer, came through the glass door. Angeline bustled towards her, plump, and slovenly, and smiling. 'So what's new, Miss Ferguson?' Angeline's tired, pudgy face was a white mask of make-up, her only brilliance was the bleached gold of her heavily teased hair.

'So what style do you want today, honey. Something special. Right? I bet you've got yourself a pretty heavy date tonight!'

'Angeline, you are just terrible!' Miss Ferguson giggled.

'Sit down and I'll shampoo you. You know what my husband says to me,

23

Miss Ferguson? – "You better keep your mouth shut, Angeline. You know too much about all the girls in the neighbourhood. You could be one of the biggest blackmailers in New York city!" '

'I just bet you could, Angeline!'

'Look at it this way, honey. You get some married woman and she's quite happy doing her own hair and messing it up for years – then one day she'll come in here and she'll say "Give me a new colour, Angeline – give me something really different". Well, you can bet your bottom dollar she's not doing it for her husband. Right? Angeline doesn't talk. You can lose customers that way. But she notices. I mean, sometimes you'll get a cute young kid, and she'll come in and tell you that she wants all her hair cut off. I know at once she's got some guy that's giving her trouble. It's crazy! But with the young kids – a guy walks out on them, and the first thing they want to do is to have every hair on their head cut off!" '

'Maybe it's psychological,' Miss Ferguson said helpfully. 'Nowadays it seems like so many things are psychological.'

'I don't know what kind of dopey thing it is, honey, but I always try to stop them doing it. I mean what fella's worth going round looking like you've just been doing a stint on a chain-gang?'

'Your kind of work must be very individual kind of work. It must be very rewarding.' Miss Ferguson's head was tilted backwards in Angeline's basin. 'I think that different people's problems are always so rewarding.'

'Sometimes they are. Sometimes they are not, Miss Ferguson. Last week I had a woman walk in here – and she sits herself down and I give her a set and I give her a manicure – and the next moment she's down on the floor, among all the pins and rollers – and she's tossing around and yelling her head off – and she's giving birth! Jesus! What a mess! And my other customers weren't crazy about it at all. She had no right coming in here if she's that far gone. Oh boy! Was I mad with her!'

'But she couldn't have wanted that to happen, Angeline. I mean, she couldn't have – like planned it – could she?'

Angeline shrugged, 'I don't know. She was a Puerto Rican – very dark hair – not tinted – real. She wasn't coloured – I don't take coloured people.'

Angeline noticed that Miss Ferguson was looking anxious. 'Look, honey, don't get so worried. They don't want to come in here any more. They wouldn't be seen dead in here now – don't kid yourself. I mean now – Black is Beautiful. Right?' Angeline laughed. 'They used to try and come in sometimes and then I always said to them: "Look, I want to be fair to you – I just *don't* understand

24

your hair." I didn't want to take their money and give them a lousy job, so I always told them they'd be far better off going to some Beauty Parlour where they were used to working with their kind of heads. I figured that was fair to them – and fair to myself. Right?'

'I guess that was fair,' Miss Ferguson said doubtfully.

'Those kind of heads need special techniques. I mean . . .' Angeline stopped her patter and her beady little puffy eyes flicked anxiously to the other end of her Beauty Salon. Suddenly there was a stir, and her clients' heads were coming craning out from under their dryers.

'What's all the excitement over there?' Miss Ferguson asked her.

'It's nothing. It's nothing,' Angeline said irritably. 'It's just Mrs Klein. I guess that the customers are starting to ask her about her tattoo.'

'Her tattoo, Angeline?'

'Well, it's not exactly a tattoo. I just don't quite know what you'd call it. I guess you'd say it's more like a brand. She's Jewish and she was in one of those camps in Germany. They did it to her there. She's got these huge, horrible, black numbers stamped the whole way down her arm.'

'Oh gee! Isn't that terrible, Angeline? Isn't that a terrible thing?'

'It's terrible alright, you oughta just take a close look at it. Yesterday when she came to answer my "ad" she was telling me that she can't wear short sleeves even in the summer. She gets all these wise-guys on the subways – and they think they are being cute. "Are you scared that you might forget your social security number, lady?" – that's what they ask her – all that kind of stupid bull.'

'Oh Jesus, Angeline! That's just terrible! But surely they don't have a clue what it is – do they? I mean no one could say that to her – not if they knew – could they?'

'No, I guess they don't know – and I must say I kind of wish that Mrs Klein hadn't let all my customers know too – if you really want to know something. Just look at them now. Just look at all their faces! I don't know what Mrs Klein's been telling them what with all the noise and the dryers blowing – but boy – they sure don't look too crazy about it. Oh boy! Has Mrs Klein upset them! You see old Mrs Craxton down at the end over there – when she came in here she was just terrific. She was really great – she was laughing – she was having herself a ball. "I have only one life, Angeline, and I want to live it as a blonde!" That's what she said to me – and she's nearly seventy. Now look at her. Jesus! She looks like she's going to pass out, or have a heart attack or something. And look at Miss Martini and Mrs Wade. They are sitting there under their dryers and they look both like they are going to their own funerals.'

'But you can't blame them, Angeline. I mean a horrible thing like that — it kind of gets you.'

'Honey.' Angeline frowned and grimly tugged her comb through Miss Ferguson's wet hair. 'I am *not* blaming the customers.'

'Have you asked Mrs Klein about her experiences, Angeline? I mean when you see a woman like that — you kind of want to ask her a lot of questions — and you kind of don't want to ask her a lot of questions. Do you know what I mean?'

'No, I haven't asked Mrs Klein any questions, Miss Ferguson — and I'm not planning to ask Mrs Klein any questions either. Maybe Mrs Klein likes to tell people things — it certainly seems like she does. But how do I know? I never set eyes on her till yesterday. All I know is that today while she's been down there at the other end of the shop doing the rinses it seems like she's been saying plenty to the customers. I can tell that just to look at them. Oh boy! You sure wouldn't know it was a Saturday. It's like she's hit them all on the head or something!'

'You'd think that there must be things that Mrs Klein could do about her arm. I mean science is so great now, Angeline. There must be operations she could have — skin-grafts — you know.'

'Look, I don't know what Mrs Klein can do about her arm, Miss Ferguson. But one thing I know — I'll be glad to close early this evening. I'm bushed today. I've just about had it. My husband's coming here soon to pick me up for a movie. Herb always wants to make a big night of it Saturdays. I feel more like going home and going right to sleep. I feel like doing that most nights really — but you know how the fellas are — you've got to keep them happy — or I guess you've got to try and have a shot at it. Anyway when you are dry, Miss Ferguson, I'm closing down the shop.'

Mrs Klein was sweeping a rubble of cigarette stubs, pins, and hair clippings off the floor. Angeline was pulling down the blinds. Perspiration poured down the exhausted faces of the two women. The over-heated air was stale with the smell of singed hair, old smoke and sickly, perfumed spray.

'Jesus! Well, I guess that's it for today, and it's Sunday tomorrow thank God!'

Angeline collapsed into a chair and stared at the great piles of dye-stained towels, the dirty ash-trays, the tattered magazines, and the innumerable bottles of lacquer, nail-polish and lotion, which lay scattered about without their tops.

'Oh boy!' Angeline looked across her Beauty Salon into one of the many mirrors and spoke to a reflection of Mrs Klein.

'Leave it! Oh for Christ's sake just leave it, Mrs Klein! You don't have to bother with all that goddam mess. Now that all the clients have gone there's something I've got to speak to you about. My husband's coming here soon to pick me up for a movie – so I guess I'll have to make it quick.'

Mrs Klein stopped sweeping and turned round. 'What do you want to say to me, Angeline?'

'Look,' Angeline coughed, 'look, I know that you've had a pretty tough time and all that – but gee, Mrs Klein – I guess I've still gotta say something to you that you won't be too crazy about.'

Mrs Klein's dark smudged eyes stared at Angeline. 'So what do you want to say?'

'Gee, Mrs Klein. I really hate to do this. I know that it may be a kind of a sensitive subject with you – but there's something I've just gotta say to you. If you want to come in to give me a hand here on Saturdays – you've really gotta keep down your sleeves.'

Mrs Klein stood very stiffly with her fingers tightly gripping the handle of her broom. 'But I only roll up my sleeves when I have to do the rinses, Angeline.'

Angeline bustled over to her and slapped her on the back. 'Gee I know that, Mrs Klein. I've been in this business for longer than I'd like to tell you. You don't need to tell Angeline why you roll up your sleeves. You think I don't know what it is to be handling these lousy dyes? But boy! I really hate to have to make a point of it like this. I mean I just love having you working here Saturdays. It's like it's a favour for you, and it's a favour for me. Right? But I have to think of the customers. You see they come to *Angeline's* because they like a kind of a comfortable atmosphere. Look, why's the place always full weekends? I mean there's pretty heavy competition in this line of business. Jesus! And I'm just not kidding you. But the girls still keep coming in here because they know that Angeline can always make them laugh, Angeline can always make them feel good. *Angeline's* is a kind of a friendly neighbourhood place and they like that. And mostly we get a pretty decent class of person coming in here. It's not often that someone with a headful of fleas comes to *Angeline's*.'

Angeline reached out nervously for one of her hair-rollers. She took a lock of her own dry over-bleached hair and rolled it deftly into a curl and sprayed it with setting-lotion.

'Look, Mrs Klein, if it was just me it would be different. I have a different point of view. I mean when we are both alone in the shop, you can roll your sleeves up all you like. You know Angeline, Mrs Klein. She's been around, she isn't going to turn a hair. She understands that you've had yourself a pretty rough deal and all that. But you know that some of my customers haven't exactly found that life's been all milk and roses either, Mrs Klein, and they come to *Angeline's* – to relax – to have a set – to have a touch up – to have themselves a ball. So when the clients come in here I was really wondering if maybe you couldn't wear some tatty old long-sleeved gown that it wouldn't matter if you got the dyes on it. You know – some lousy old overall that who gives a damn if it gets a bit wet.'

'No, Angeline,' Mrs Klein shook her head, 'no, I certainly don't see myself working with wet sleeves dripping all over the customers' faces.'

'Gee, Mrs Klein, I guess you are right. Maybe that wouldn't be too practical. Oh boy! I really hate to say all this to you. But it's just the customers. You know what I mean, Mrs Klein. In this business you have to keep thinking about the customers. You are stuck with them. Right? And you see when you are giving a client a rinse, Mrs Klein – your arms are so near them. That's the real problem.' Angeline was starting to stutter. 'I mean – like – your arms are really in their face. Look,' she said quickly, 'it's not the thing itself. I mean the thing itself doesn't look so bad. I mean it's just a bunch of numbers. But it's the idea. You can understand that. And if the customers aren't comfortable – you can't be comfortable. You know that, Mrs Klein.'

'I don't quite understand what you want me to do, Angeline.'

'Look, Mrs Klein. You seem like a very nice woman – a very serious type of person. And it seems like you've gotten yourself a good European education which is more than most of us. So you know what I really think, Mrs Klein? You are just wasting yourself here. Yes, Mrs Klein – that's what I think, even if I seem to be speaking against my own shop. You oughta get yourself something with a future like.'

'So you don't want me to help out here next Saturday, Angeline?'

'Gee, Mrs Klein – I'm not saying that, Mrs Klein. All I'm trying to say is that it would be better for you – not for me – but for you – if you got yourself some kind of weekend work that could really get you places.'

'If that's how you feel, Angeline.' Mrs Klein went to get her coat and hat.

'I'd like to settle what I owe you, Mrs Klein.' Angeline rumbled feverishly in her pocket and brought out a few dollars. She started forward to hand them to Mrs Klein, but lost her nerve and put them down on the side of a basin.

Mrs Klein looked at the money, hesitated, and then decided to ignore it, and she started walking slowly out of the Beauty Salon through the rows of Angeline's unoccupied, old, battered hair dryers which stood like desolate science-fiction equipment abandoned somewhere in space.

'I hope that you'll drop by and see us some time, Mrs Klein. I'll always be glad to give you some high-lights or a set. I won't charge you. You know that.'

Mrs Klein seemed not to have heard.

'Mrs Klein! You know that one of my clients was saying today that there are wonderful operations you can have nowadays. Have you ever thought of having an operation – a skin-graft, Mrs Klein?'

'I've had a lot of operations. I'm not having any more operations, Angeline.'

As Mrs Klein went out through the glass door, a big-shouldered, hearty man with a crew-cut and a very heavy jaw pushed past her and came into the shop.

'Hi honey! What's going on? Why are you looking so worried? Was that one of the customers I just saw going out? Has she been giving you trouble? What's her problem? She didn't like her hair? She looked all het up.'

'That wasn't one of the customers, Herb. That was the woman that I got to help out Saturdays. I just fired her.'

'You just fired her, Angeline!'

Herb shrugged and threw out his huge arms in a gesture of despair. 'What the Hell did you do that for, honey? You know you've been losing a helluva lot of custom the way things have been going Saturdays, and you've been just knocking yourself out.'

Angeline sat down in front of one of her mirrors and mechanically started to tease her bright bleached fringe.

'Wouldn't you know it!' she said, 'wouldn't you know that Angeline would have all the luck! I mean listen to this, Herb. Just how many people try to get someone to help them out Saturdays in their Beauty Salon, and they get a woman turning up with big, black, concentration camp numbers stamped the whole way down her arm? I mean can you beat that, Herb? Isn't that just about the end?'

'Is that why you fired her, Angey?' Herb's heavy-jawed face became suddenly very red. 'You must be kidding, Angeline! You fired someone just because they have a few numbers on their arms? I just don't get it. Are you out of your mind? How come you did a crazy thing like that?'

'Look, Herb,' Angeline said irritably, 'just don't start on me now for Christ's sake! I feel like I've really had it today, and I don't need you to put on the Big-Hearted-Joe act, and all that crap. I'm trying to run a Beauty Parlour – get it? I'm not the Salvation Army. I'm trying to run a Beauty Parlour – so get that through your thick skull, Herb honey!'

'I don't get it, Angeline.'

Herb's face became even redder and he glared at his wife's hair dryers as though they were an enemy. 'I just don't understand how your mind works, Angeline. Every Saturday you come running to me complaining – "Herb, I feel just knocked out" – "Herb, the shop's really killing me." Every Saturday you say you are too tired to enjoy a movie – and too tired to enjoy anything else too – and you know damn well what I'm talking about. And then you get someone to help you out Saturdays – someone who knows the work – and the first thing you do is to go and fire them for some goddam stupid reason which is all up in your own head.'

Herb kicked a copy of *Vogue* which was lying on the floor. 'I don't know, honey,' he muttered, 'but boy, you better watch it! Don't come to me next Saturday telling me that you feel like you can't hardly stand up. Sometimes I think that you just try to make yourself exhausted, Angeline, and a guy can get pretty fed up with that kind of crap. To have to live with someone who always feels tired all the time – I mean Jesus! What kind of a life's that for anyone?'

Herb gave the *Vogue* another kick. 'I'm just telling you something, Angeline. Just don't count on me too much – and boy I really mean that. A guy who works late most nights of the week wants someone who isn't too tired to enjoy things Saturdays. And one of these days he might just say to Hell with it – and go and find himself someone else – someone who feels like they can stand up!'

Angeline slumped in her chair and held her head with its tall helmet of teased golden hair in her hands. 'For Christ's sake, Herb – lay off me, can't you? Why are you always like that, Herb? Why do you always have to hit a person when they are down? Don't get mad at me, Herb. Look, I'll get someone else for Saturdays – I mean I guess I will. You know when you have something happen to you like I did today – it's funny – but you kind of lose your confidence. You start to think that everyone's going to have something the matter, so that you can't possibly keep them. I couldn't keep that woman today. Please, Herb – be fair. You're the one who's always telling me that I've got to make

Angeline's into the kind of place where all the girls can come in and just die laughing.'

Angeline waved her plump little dye-stained hands as she pleaded with her husband. 'Look – use your nut, Herb. If you had seen that woman's arm – you wouldn't be so mad at me. Of course I said to her that it didn't look so bad. I mean you have to say that – don't you? But Jesus, Herb! You should have seen the size of her numbers. They were like something you see on the backsides of a bunch of cattle. And it wasn't only her brand either. Her whole arm looked all kind of horrible and shrivelled like they'd done something to her muscle. I mean Christ, Herb! You could get a customer and she just wants to relax and have her hair shampooed – and she might take a look at that arm and it would really turn her stomach. And, well, she might just figure like – who really needs it?'

'Okay. Okay. Who needs it? I'm sorry I blew my top. Please just forget it, and for Christ's sake don't let's spend the whole evening talking about it, Angeline.' Herb came and sat down next to his wife and put his heavy arm round her shoulder. Angeline tried to push away his arm.

'Look, don't start messing me around, Herb. I don't feel like it right now. I don't feel like it at all. I must have been out of my mind to take that woman. If only I'd never taken her, Herb – I'd never have had to fire her. Oh boy!'

'Well, don't get yourself so excited, Angeline,' Herb kissed his wife's cheek. 'Maybe she didn't mind too much when you fired her. What were you paying her anyway? I know your Beauty Parlour means everything to you, Angeline. But Jesus honey, it isn't everyone who feels they'll just die if they can't work in your shop.'

Angeline's tired face twitched. 'Oh Herb,' she said impatiently, 'that's so like you to say that – just so goddam stupid. Mrs Klein minded – she minded alright. And you know something funny Herb? Mrs Klein didn't mean too much to me when she first came in to work here. I only really started to feel something for her when I saw her walking out – all kind of bent, and red in the face, and upset.'

Herb shrugged his huge shoulders. 'Look, let's face it, Angeline. Maybe you are like that. Maybe you never really start to feel anything for anyone – not till you've got them walking out – just like you say – all kind of bent, and red in the face, and upset.'

'Please Herb, I don't need your cute wise-cracks. They don't make me laugh.'

'I'm not kidding, Angeline. I'm not really kidding at all.'

Angeline made an exasperated gesture with her fat little hands. 'I don't

31

know why you sound as though that makes it better, Herb. It just makes it quite a bit worse. But I'm not thinking about you right now, Herb. I'm thinking about Mrs Klein. I sort of keep feeling that I didn't fire her very nicely. I guess she got me rattled. It was the way she kept staring at me with those great black eyes. She kind of made me say things to her that I never should have said.'

Herb pushed his tongue into the side of his cheek as though he was sucking a gum-drop. 'You sound like you're blaming her, Angeline. I know you love blaming people. I mean I'm just used to you always blaming me honey. But to blame this poor old buzzard Mrs Klein – isn't that a bit much?'

'I'm not blaming her. Oh Jesus, Herb! Why are you always such a nit? I'm just saying that if she hadn't kept staring like that, I feel that I could have done the whole thing – sort of much better.'

Herb gave his wife's back a tolerant clap. 'Look, it's not all that easy to fire anyone nicely, Angeline. So forget Mrs Klein – forget the whole business. It was just one of those things.'

'It certainly was, Herb.' Angeline shook her head and rolled her eyes up to the ceiling. 'You should have seen what happened here today in the shop. Oh boy! Did Mrs Klein louse up the atmosphere! And I just can't let that happen, Herb. Look – don't kid around – you need the shop – and I need the shop. What are you getting every week Herb? A guy who's nearly fifty and he's working as a soda-jerk – what's he ever going to get? I mean Jesus Herb! We're not getting any younger. Sometimes when I wake up in the night everything really scares me. The shop's all we've got. I've knocked myself out for the shop. I just can't let anything hurt the shop.'

'Okay. Okay.' Herb again kissed his wife's cheek. 'The way things are going – gee – I guess you may be right. You certainly understand the Beauty business better than I do, Angey. I guess it's a woman's world and a guy can really get lost in that set-up. So let's just both relax a bit, Angeline. And for Christ's sake let's forget about that woman. Okay – so she didn't work out. Okay – so you fired her. I mean she's gone, hasn't she? So why waste the whole evening beefing about it? You've got what you wanted.'

'Oh boy!' Angeline shook her head, 'when you say things like that, Herb, sometimes I wonder if you understand anything at all.'

'Then forget it. I keep telling you I'm just sick to death of talking about the whole business. Relax. Oh, for Christ's sake relax, Angeline. Look – it's Saturday baby! Let's go out and have a few drinks and try to have ourselves a ball. Gee! You know something? I just love your hair today, Angey. It really looks terrific. One thing about a wife who's a professional – she never lets you get tired of her hair. It always looks great and it's never the same two days running! And boy, it smells pretty good too. It's crazy, Angeline! Your hair always kind of excites me!'

Herb leaned over and whispered in his wife's ear. 'You know what I'd like to do, Angey? I'd like to come in your hair. I'd like to come in your hair right now baby!'

Angeline suddenly started to cry. Her husband quickly stroked her brilliant dry gold hair. 'For Christ's sake! What's the matter with you, Angey? I guess you're still upset because I acted so unpleasant when you first told me you'd fired that character. You know I didn't mean what I said about finding myself a new woman for Saturdays. I only said that because I was so mad at you. You know how I really feel about you, Angey. Do you want to feel how hard you've made me right now. Just put your hand on me. Sometimes I get like that just thinking about you. You've got nothing to cry for, Angeline. Most wives start complaining when they've been married as long as you have, Angey. But boy! You sure can't complain about me, Angeline. I still want to screw you just as much as I ever did. All my mother's people are Italians – so I guess I'm kind of hot-blooded. I just wish that your goddam shop didn't make you feel so tired all the time. And Jesus! I wish you'd put your hand on me now, honey. You've got me so hotted up!'

Angeline wiped her eyes with a handkerchief. 'Look, Herb – I told you already the shop's all I've got. And today everything's been so lousy here in the shop – that I don't feel like putting my hand anywhere. Can't you get that?'

Angeline blew her nose, and her exhausted little swollen eyes stared aggressively at her husband. 'You know something, Herb? You're so hooked on the idea that you're so hot-blooded, and special, and Italian, that you just never seem to take it in that sometimes a person can have something quite different on their mind. Okay – so you've got yourself all hard, Herb. Okay – so you've got yourself all hotted up. But who needs it, Herb? Who needs it?'

Angeline tried to get up from her chair. 'Oh Hell now, Herb! Don't start pulling me around for Christ's sake – and get your big face out of my face! Jesus, Herb! Now take it easy. What's the matter with you? You know we can't do it here in the shop. Now just lay off for God's sake – and get your great paws off me – and let me breathe! Don't you understand I don't feel tired – but I don't feel like doing it right now – I don't feel like doing it at all. Right now, Herb – I need you to screw me – just about like I need a hole in the head. I feel so kind of shook up.'

C

Angeline wrenched herself away from her husband and tears which were black with mascara trickled down her tired, pudgy cheeks. 'Look – find yourself someone new, Herb. I'm not stopping you. I've never tried to stop you. But go ahead and do it, Herb. Don't just keep talking about it – and don't kid around. I know you think that you're such a big ballsy guy that all the girls are after you – but you've got a face like a Virginia ham, Herb – and your belly is starting to spill all over your belt – and it sure doesn't look like you're going to be the next President yet. So be a bit realistic – and cut out all the crap. It isn't everybody that's going to be so crazy for you, Herb. And I want to know – *who*? I want to know – just exactly *who* – you are ever going to find? Please don't put on that act with me again, honey. I don't have the patience. And boy – I'm telling you something – you've got to lay off me today, Herb. I feel very bad today. I feel very bad indeed. And I just wish that you could get that through your great big hot-blooded head. It was that woman turning up like that. Wouldn't you know it would have to happen to Angeline? And wouldn't you know she'd end up making me feel like a lousy son of a bitch? Oh boy!'

'Oh to Hell with that woman! To Hell with your shop!' Herb jumped up and started pacing agitatedly up and down the aisle formed by his wife's hairdriers. 'Your shop certainly always comes first with you, Angeline. Jesus Christ Almighty!'

Herb suddenly noticed the money that Mrs Klein had left. 'And what the fuck are those dollar bills doing there on that basin? Oh Jesus! I get it . . . I think I really get it. You get dollars for your tips – and I just get dimes and quarters. I guess that's one more thing for you to throw in my face, Angeline. Jesus Christ Almighty!'

'Cut out the sob-stuff, Herb.' Angeline started to tidy her hair. 'I just don't feel like telling you about that money. But you know something useful you can do, my big Herb honey? You can fetch me that lousy little pile of dough – and then we're getting the Hell out of here I'm telling you. You know what I need? All that I need right now is a very stiff drink, Herb. Oh boy! Everything just stinks and it seems like some people have all the luck.'

THE BABY NURSE

He was abject in the way he persistently tried to placate her. She always called him 'Mr Richardson' and he hardly recognised his own name when he heard her use it. She always managed to make 'Mr Richardson' sound like something so infinitely shoddy and disappointing – something that only the unfairness of life had forced her to contend with.

'Can I make you a cup of tea, Miss Renny?' he would ask her.

'I could most certainly do with a cup of tea, Mr Richardson.' And she made it so plain that she felt not a grain of gratitude for his tea-making, that she saw it as only one more pathetic inadequate gesture which only served to remind her of the immensity of the debt that he owed her.

Sometimes when they had meals together and he was listening with slavish sympathy to all her complaints, feeling half-suffocated by his own sycophancy as he flattered and cajoled her, suddenly Miss Renny would seem like an innocent. He felt certain that her immense vanity would never permit her to suspect the intensity of the venomous hate he often felt for her. He found he could get some small sour satisfaction just from sensing his own power to deceive her. He felt that she deserved to be deceived by him for he could never forgive her for the way she had originally fooled him. He had been glad when she first arrived. When he had got back from the hospital with his wife he had felt actively relieved when Miss Renny's bulky form had arrived with a suitcase and installed itself in his flat. He could never forgive Miss Renny for having originally tricked him by what he now felt was the sheer fraudulence of all her fat.

Miss Renny was certainly a woman of the most deceptive obesity, for the very plumpness of all the roly-poly flesh that covered her huge frame conveyed a comforting and erroneous first-impression that she was cheerful, kindly and maternal.

A professionally trained baby nurse, Miss Renny carried her overweight with great panache and managed to present it with pride to the world as if she felt it to be her greatest strength. But as the days went by and Stephen Richardson found himself forced to eat more and more meals alone with her, he was very soon to learn that Miss Renny's trust-inspiring corpulence was the most glaring symptom of her main weakness. Miss Renny was extremely greedy. Meats, and cakes and puddings, excited her. She thought about them. She plotted in order to get herself very large shares of them. It was as if all the calories that Miss Renny loved to consume fired her blood like adrenalin, for despite her amazing bulk she was aggressively energetic and active. As his wife Arabella had seemed to shrink as she lay all day crying in her bed like a quivering little jelly of ineptitude, so Miss Renny had seemed to swell until she filled the whole flat with her combative and competitive competence.

'What's wrong with you? Can I do anything to help?' He kept asking Arabella the same questions until they seemed as monotonous as her refusal to give anything except a choked gulp for an answer.

'Please just leave me alone. I might feel better if I was left alone . . .'

He would see that his wife's spongy, tear-swollen eyes were cursing him for his lack of sympathy and comprehension. He found that he was glad to leave her alone, for she seemed malevolent lying there on her crumpled unmade bed, with an agonised and defensive glare in her eye, looking so oddly ravaged and sluttish. She reminded him of a miser in the way she was stubbornly hoarding some great sack of unshareable hostility.

And all the time Miss Renny had gone flouncing round his flat in a cloud of baby-powder and self-congratulation. As if she were inebriated by a sense of her own indispensability, she rollicked around, boiling up her formulas, rinsing out tiny cardigans and bootees. She loudly hummed lullabyes as she sterilised with her vast steel sterilising equipment. Every day she went trundling out on shopping expeditions, puffing, as she pushed the unwieldy pram, and she bought herself more and more cakes and pies and nappy-pins.

'And who is meant to get Mrs Richardson all her meals? I have my hands full . . .' Miss Renny's eyes would taunt him. They reminded him of two little malicious currants fraudulently nestling under the protective camouflage of the cherubic chubbiness of her rosy-apple cheeks. He sensed that she was only too delighted by the unusual situation which was prevailing in his household and that all her immense energies were directing themselves to finding shrewd ways by which she could best exploit it.

'Don't you worry about my wife's meals, Miss Renny. You just devote yourself to the baby.'

His wife refused to have any meals. When he got back in the evenings from his office he would bring her honey and toast, which she would nibble with apathetic and distracted disgust as if it were some dangerous repellent substance which, in typical bad faith, he was forcing on her.

'Why don't you have a strong whisky. If you don't want to eat you might find that a drink would make you feel better.'

'It's as if an ink-fish had squirted black poisons into my brain. Alcohol would only make me feel worse. All you can do is leave me alone.'

'Didn't you want to have the child? You should have told me that you didn't want to. Surely you didn't have it just to please me . . .' The infant seemed to be so painfully associated with the despairing state of mind which had followed its birth that at the very mention of its name his wife would immediately go into a choking attack of wild weak sobbing. He would stand by her bed ineptly trying to soothe her until, finding it useless, he would go next door and, in an attempt to curb his exasperation, he would make cocoa for Miss Renny.

He sent for Arabella's doctor, who said that her condition was a common one and that she would snap out of it if she rested.

'It's just the old post-natals!'

The doctor prescribed some pills which had no effect on her behaviour. She went on spending her days shut up in her room, and whenever Stephen went in to visit her he found her lying staring at the bleak grey eye of her unturned-on television as if she were watching some invisible horror movie.

'You will be pleased to hear that Miss Renny has got the little Miss off the night-feed, Mr Richardson! It's all experience . . .' Miss Renny was always talking about her 'experience'. She made it sound like something that only she, by her superior nature, possessed, something magical that she carried on her portly person like an amulet to ward off the evil influences which would plunge the household into ruin if it were ever removed. Occasionally he felt a sinking faith in the saving powers of Miss Renny's experience, although he always tried to squash these doubts, like a believer who feels imperilled by the needle-jabs of his own thoughts. Sometimes he found himself wondering whether Miss Renny was so over-interested in feeding herself that she was starving the baby. For night and day the infant never seemed to stop screaming. As if the despairing mood of its mother had been instilled at birth into its tiny bones, it filled the whole flat with its wails.

'Its only wind,' Miss Renny would chirp. Sometimes she said it was being naughty.

'If you want to start a family Mr Richardson – you are going to have to get used to crying.'

As weeks went by he started to resent Arabella for her unlifting despondency and saw it less as a disease than a desertion. She seemed to have selfishly sailed away on the tides of her own depression and he felt stunned and bitter that she had left him to cope alone with his dispiriting little household, composed of Miss Renny and the howling bundle which was the baby.

It was the dinners which he felt obliged to eat with Miss Renny in the kitchen which he found the most agonising experience of the day. Miss Renny had a breast which hardly seemed to be a breast it was so like some great boulder jutting out under her white nurse's uniform. It was as if, with her intensely competitive nature, Miss Renny had felt the need, in all her years of playing a professional maternal role, to grow herself such a monumental breast that she could trust it to dwarf and out-rival all competing breasts. Miss Renny loved to chatter while she ate, and as she talked, she had a habit of thrusting out her great breast, and often she pushed it so close to his mouth that he was sorely tempted to bite it.

'Well, I must say that Mrs Richardson doesn't seem to be all that thrilled by her lovely little baby girl. I don't think she's bothered to take one peep at the poor little mite since she brought it back from the hospital. I've been doing this kind of work for years, Mr Richardson, but I have to tell you frankly that I've never seen a mother like that . . . My problem was always trying to keep the young mothers *away* from the babies . . . All day and all night I do nothing except devote myself to your little child, Mr Richardson. But sometimes I look at that dear little girl when she is sleeping and I find I can't stop myself from thinking that it might have been better for her if she had been still-born . . .'

'You have to understand that my wife is not at all well, Miss Renny.'

'Mrs Richardson is a very young woman. I'm afraid I can have no patience with that kind of self-pampering laziness. She can hardly hope to get her strength back if she wants to spend her days lying flat on her back and playing the lady of leisure. All my other mothers were up on their feet a few hours after the delivery . . .'

He disliked discussing Arabella with Miss Renny and found he could only steer her away from this topic which deeply intrigued her if he encouraged her to speak of the other families she had worked for. She would then boast interminably of how they had all loved and depended on her.

'I've never known a family where I haven't been able to leave my mark,' Miss Renny kept repeating. And he found he always had an instant image of all Miss Renny's families lying in stricken position with their gashed mouths biting the earth like village victims of some barbaric machine-gun massacre.

He would sit silently nodding encouragement and coughing with monotonous courtesy while Miss Renny chattered. He would note with nausea the pleasure she took in her food, listen to her breathing as it became heavy, almost lustful, as she took off the cover of a dish of stew and sniffed it.

'When I was with Lady Eccleston, Mr Richardson, I was always treated exactly as if I was part of the family. We often used to sit down sixteen for dinner. Oh, that was nothing for us! Sir Keith was in the government, so we always entertained a lot of cabinet ministers. What a charming bunch of fascinating men they all were too! The baby was Ronald . . . They still send me photos of him. How his mother doted on him! That was a family that made you feel glad to be alive . . .'

Even though his dinners with Miss Renny depressed and bored him to distraction he found himself often deliberately prolonging them. Every night he kept putting off the moment when he would have to go and sleep in Arabella's room. It seemed to him that their bedroom had acquired an unpleasantly sour and stagnant smell as if the malignancy of his wife's mood had permeated its very atmosphere. He disliked lying beside her when she huddled there so inert and rigid on the very edge of the bed that he felt she was bracing herself for some dreaded attack. Sometimes he tried to talk to her but she only answered with a little sniff or a sob. She reminded him of the infant, she seemed so speechless, lying there in the darkness tightly swaddled in her own moroseness. He found that her insomnia was infectious, and every night he found it almost impossible to get to sleep feeling his wife's tension to be something eerie and terrifying, like something he had once read about in a ghost story, a headless clammy lady who entered beds at midnight and snuggled between the sheets.

One evening he set up a camp-bed for himself in the little windowless storage-room which was beside the kitchen. The only other bedroom in the flat was occupied by Miss Renny and the baby. He found the cold and uncomfortable isolation of the storage-room a relief. He could sense that his presence was becoming more and more painful to Arabella, that it pressured her to a point she found intolerable. As if she felt a certain shame at her own distressed behaviour, she appeared to be acutely sensitive to his unvoiced resentment at her collapse. If he made any attempt to cheer her it merely seemed to aggravate her guilt which in turn aggravated her gloom. As if she were cowering away from his criticism, the very sight of him now seemed to make her retreat even further into the weird weepy world of her own melancholia.

Miss Renny was displeasingly over-interested in his storage-room move. She offered to help him make up the camp-bed and made him feel there was a symbolic importance to her gesture, for in general she categorically refused to do any housework unless it pertained directly to the baby. She had been insisting lately that he employ a cleaning-woman to work full-time in the flat.

'In all my other households I was never expected to be a drudge. I certainly never cooked for myself. I took responsibility for their child and they treated my work with respect. But then all my other families considered that their infant was a gift from God . . .'

Miss Renny managed to insinuate that she assumed that it was at his wife's insistence that he had been forced to move out from her bed.

'Any woman who cries like that all day,' he heard Miss Renny murmuring to the bonneted ear of the infant, 'she must be crying for some reason.'

On other occasions Miss Renny took a very different view of Arabella's conduct.

'I think you are wonderful the way you put up with it, Mr Richardson.'

'Put up with what, Miss Renny?'

He would stare across the kitchen table and the creases of Miss Renny's double chins would look like cruel secondary smiles which were underlining her real smile.

'None of my other husbands would have allowed their wives to get away with murder.'

'Get away with murder?' He had acquired a dismal habit of dumbly repeating all her sentences in order to gain time to brace himself for the stab of her coming remarks.

'Murder doesn't have to be committed with a knife, Mr Richardson. But you seem to be a little too weak to face up to that. I know you like to play the patient understanding husband. That's all very charming and touching. But the whole burden of this miserable household is falling on me. Quite frankly, Mr Richardson, I don't know how long I will be able to take it . . . I've always been a very cheerful type of person and it takes a lot to get me down. But you feel that the unhappiness in this flat is as thick as porridge and you could eat it with a spoon. I'm afraid it's affecting my health . . . I've always

40

been very sensitive to the atmosphere of the places where I work. I just have to take care of my health . . . I've had to work hard all my life. I've never been able to afford to retire to my bed and throw my responsibilities on to other people like a certain young woman we both know . . .'

He doubled Miss Renny's salary, cravenly submitting to her duplicitous blackmail, for although he dreaded the very sight of her sitting in his kitchen like an over-fed Brittania ruling her invisible waves, he was perversely tortured by an almost primitive terror that she might suddenly leave. When he was in his office in the daytime he was persistently nagged by an anxiety that in his absence Miss Renny might have some unfortunate interchange with Arabella and that he would find when he got back to the flat that she had seized up her suitcase and left. Although he sometimes found himself identifying with the infant and often felt incensed by Arabella's refusal to register the remotest interest in its existence, he also had a terror that he might suddenly find himself forced to handle it. He had such an exaggerated idea of its fragility that he feared that if he was left just one night alone with it, he would somehow manage to snap its frail life-thread by some clumsy masculine ineptitude.

Almost as much as he dreaded finding himself in charge of the infant, he now dreaded being left alone in the flat with his wife. Oppressive as he found the obese and overbearing presence of Miss Renny, at least Miss Renny talked, at least Miss Renny would eat.

'I've always been in love with gorgeous materials,' Arabella had once said to him.

'Marvellous silks and satins and furs excite me. Whenever I get the chance to wear them I just can't stop stroking myself. If I see a photograph of myself wearing something fabulous I find myself secretly kissing the photograph.'

Now he felt she had self-indulgently wrapped herself up in her new wretchedness in much the same way that she had once loved to wrap herself up in silks, and satins, and furs. He felt chilled by the sight of her perpetually closed door, exasperated by the way she was so concentrated on her own condition that she seemed to have lost all desire to improve it.

'Naturally you are depressed, shut up in this room all day by yourself. For Christ's sake get up, meet people, go out!'

'I don't want to get up, meet people, go out.'

He knew she had started to drink by herself and this disturbed and wounded him, for she always irritably refused any drink he offered her. Her refusal to drink with him seemed to express an aggressive refusal to share anything. Miss Renny would show him the depleted sunken whisky bottles.

'I see that a little bird has been sneaking out in the night, Mr Richardson . . .'

Miss Renny had started drinking rather heavily herself. She now drank the best part of a bottle of vodka every night before dinner, claiming that she needed it medicinally to enable her to breathe in an unhappy household. Sensing the vulnerability of his position, she exploited his reliance on her by ordering herself more and more expensive foods and wines which she charged to his account. If he had once found it unattractive to watch Miss Renny's false teeth snapping up her stew, he found it now far more painful to watch without protest while she went gobbling through great plates of smoked salmon and paté. All the hocks and clarets that Miss Renny sipped with her supper in no way seemed to mellow her, rather they seemed to release her animosity. She grumbled incessantly. She complained that the plug of the kitchen kettle was inconvenient – that her bedroom was traffic-noisy – that the water in his taps was so hard that it was chapping her hands. She complained that she felt bored when he left to go to his office in the daytime.

'I've always been a fun-loving person. And whatever you want to say about Mrs Richardson – you could hardly call her very scintillating company . . .' In the evenings when he dined with her in the kitchen Miss Renny made it more and more obvious that she missed the company of cabinet ministers.

Although Miss Renny loved to complain of her *ennui* when she was left alone in the flat in the daytime, he suspected that she found many ways to divert herself and that she spent a good deal of her day tormenting Arabella and doing her best to increase his wife's feeling of inadequacy and gloom. Sometimes Miss Renny dropped little hints of her daytime activities.

'I went into Mrs Richardson's bedroom and I had a little word with her this morning. "What a selfish young woman you are!" That's what I said to her. "You have a devoted young husband and you don't care what your disgusting behaviour is doing to him. And as for your poor little helpless baby girl . . . I find you inhuman. I'm afraid I just find you positively inhuman."'

'Yes, yes Miss Renny. Shall we see if there is anything on the television?'

Arabella never once mentioned Miss Renny. But then she spoke less and less. When he visited her she often hardly seemed to be aware that he was in the room.

'Every day Mrs Richardson looks worse!' Miss Renny would tell him triumphantly every night when he got home. 'I suppose Mrs Richardson must have been quite a good-looking young woman when you married her. I imagine that must have been the reason why you married her. But oh dear, now! Oh poor Mrs Richardson! Her hair is just hanging down in strings of grease. Her bones are sticking out like a Belsen victim. And then she has this goofy mournful expression as if she can't take anything in. When a woman loses all pride in herself you have to feel sorry for her. They never seem to recover from the havoc it wreaks on their looks."

If Miss Renny spent most of her day teasing and needling his wife, he found he no longer very much cared. He was starting to find Arabella rather monstrous, she appeared to be so totally indifferent to anything except her inner depressive pain-signals. He found her callous that she cared so little what she mangled with her remorseless melancholia.

He had worked for some years in the same publishing house, but never before had his office seemed like such a glittering dome of pleasure. After he had received the hail of Miss Renny's conversation at breakfast, the tinkle of every telephone, the tap of every typewriter, sounded like sublime music. In his office no one said that an ink-fish had squirted black poison into their brain, and the only moments that jarred him were when the typists complimented him on the birth of his baby.

He would lunch in restaurants with friends, but whenever Arabella was mentioned he said she was very well. He found himself reluctant to describe her state of mind as if it might in some way be considered to reflect badly on himself. The dismal closeness of his relationship with Miss Renny he also wanted to hide from the world as if it were some disgraceful sore. He was very careful to avoid asking any of his friends to come to the flat. He had no wish for them to see the way that he spent far more time with Miss Renny than he spent with his wife. He had no wish for them to see the way he sat so passively in the kitchen making no protest at all while Miss Renny ventriloquised for the baby. She would press its bald frail skull against her huge thrusting breast and rock it to and fro while she spoke in a piping squeaky voice,

'I went into my Mummy's room today, Daddy. Miss Renny had given me my lovely bath and I was such a nice clean girl, all pretty and rosy. I'm afraid my Mummy's room was all nasty and smelly. Miss Renny says my Mummy has refused to change the sheets of her bed or allow her room to be cleaned ever since I was born. Miss Renny said it worried her to take me into such an unhygienic room and she hoped it wouldn't give me germs. Anyway I was looking as pretty as can be and all powdered. And I really thought my Mummy would be very pleased to see me. But do you know what she did to my nice Miss Renny? She said horrible things and she swore . . . "Just take it away,

43

you old bitch!" That's what my Mummy said to my kind Miss Renny. "For Christ's sake take it away!" '

And while Miss Renny was giving it words, he would stare at the infant and find himself unable to take his eyes off its nose. The infant's nose was the only distinctive feature in the amorphous pucker of its wizened little face. As if gazing into a distorting mirror he would see his own nose, a nose which had always seemed to him to be like a house of classical proportions whose elegant façade had been disfigured by the addition of an unsightly wing. So often when he was shaving he had looked at the unnecessary little bulge which lay at the end of his nose and felt tempted to remove it with his razor. And seeing a tiny version of his nose on the baby he felt a pity for it and, as if searching for a concrete object which he could blame as the cause of Arabella's depression, he would feel certain that his wife, ever since the birth of the child, had felt secretly saddened by the sight of its nose. He found it only too easy to imagine that someone like Arabella who was so concerned with the appearance of things might very well feel a despair at the prospect of bringing up this girl who could never be pretty because she had inherited his nose.

'She's the dead spit of her Dad!' Miss Renny loved to warble.

And always he felt a kind of panic and wished he knew of some way to offer restitution to his wife and daughter. He often found himself compulsively thinking about the infant's nose while Miss Renny was telling him about her great dream. She hoped one day to retire and buy herself a cottage of her own by the sea. Such a dream in someone else he might have found quite sympathetic. But hearing about it from Miss Renny, all he felt was disgust, for he saw it as the dream of a burglar. He always had a displeasing image of Miss Renny retiring to her sea cottage with all the spoils that she had thievishly extracted from all the households she had cunningly entered on her baby-nurse cat-ladder.

Sometimes in the middle of the night, lying alone and restless in the storage-room listening to the soft pad of Arabella's feet as she slyly crept out from her room to get herself a bottle of whisky from the kitchen, he would decide to get another nurse to replace Miss Renny. He found that this decision could distract him from the indecision that most plagued him. Should he lock up all the alcohol in the house? Or were her lonely bedroom whiskys the only thing which was now preventing Arabella from becoming suicidal?

By morning his decision to get rid of Miss Renny would fade and become a fantasy. The unexpectedness of his wife's collapse had left him with a feeling of apathetic exhaustion and he felt incapable of making the effort to find a new nurse. In his pessimistic mood, he was certain that he was bound to select some woman who would have all Miss Renny's disagreeable qualities, plus the additional defect of being dangerously incompetent.

Miss Renny sensed the security of her position in his household and became increasingly demanding and aggressive. She had engaged an aged Scottish lady as a full-time cleaner for the flat and she treated this woman who was far older and frailer than herself with a nagging tyranny. Familiarity had made Miss Renny feel that she had the freedom to treat Stephen Richardson as if she were his long-suffering wife. She accused him of taking very little interest in the baby's routines. She complained that he was so withdrawn and silent, and distracted.

'I've always liked the kind of man who has something to say for himself – the kind that can make you laugh.' She accused him of being unpopular.

'All my other families were very much in demand. They all had masses of fascinating friends who were always popping in and out for a drink and a giggle. In this household you feel so ostracised you might as well be in a leper colony.'

When Miss Renny referred to Arabella it was with more and more spite.

'I'm afraid our dear Mrs Richardson is a complete sham. If she didn't drink so much she wouldn't be any iller than the rest of us – she's the sort of woman who thinks she is so good-looking she deserves to be a duchess and then things don't quite turn out the way she hoped. So what does her ladyship do? She retires to her bed and it's boo hoo hoo!'

Sometimes he found himself weakly trying to defend Arabella and he would try to tell Miss Renny what his wife had been like before she became ill. But as he talked he would start to have the feeling that the gay clever girl he was describing was just as fictional as Miss Renny's gilded pictures of all her other families. Miss Renny and himself would seem like two tired old sailors sitting there spinning their bragging yarns. It was as if they were both trying to drug themselves against their futureless, discouraging present by hallucinating glamorous pasts. With his wife lying there so nearby in a semi-coma of drink and despondency, it seemed futile to try to make her image dance for this spiteful old woman with her sceptical fat-encrusted little eyes.

'My wife is a very talented young actress, Miss Renny.'

'Your wife is certainly a talented actress, Mr Richardson. I've been watching her perform for quite a few months now. I feel like going to the box-office and asking for my money back . . .'

Often it seemed to him that Miss Renny might go on living with him forever. He found it only too easy to visualise a fearful future in which he would
always go on leaning on Miss Renny and pandering to her caprice, eternally
doomed to her stifling domination by the apathy and cowardice which had
prevented him from getting rid of her from the start.

And then one day, quite suddenly, he struck out at Miss Renny. As he committed his vengeful act of aggression against her he was surprised by his feeling of the utter inevitability of his action. It was as if, ever since she had first
moved into his flat, in some buried way he had always been planning one day
to strike the blow which he knew would jolt her to the very core of her bulky
frame which had fattened itself for so long on his food. As he came through
the door of his flat at midnight, drunk, and staggering, and deliberately trying
to wake up the infant, he had a feeling of exhilaration from the enormity of
his act of aggression against Miss Renny. As he held on to the arm of the
blonde girl who was with him he found that his fingers were tightening on
her sleeve as if he were gripping some sharp sword.

If, by sleeping with another woman in the flat, he was striking at Arabella,
he could see her only as an accidental side-victim. His wife was so depressed
already that he felt it would hardly matter all that much to her if she were
given extra grounds for her depression.

It was Miss Renny whom he hoped to outrage by his infidelity. He wanted
to force her to be an unwilling accomplice in an act that he knew she would
consider atrocious. If the crude tastelessness of his sexual behaviour appalled
her, he wanted her to realise that she was in no position to do anything about
it. Miss Renny must be forced to realise, whatever it cost her in terms of
anguish, that in his household she was in charge of the infant, but she was
not in charge of morals.

He knew Miss Renny quite well enough to know that her man-hate would
make her feel a feverish identification with Arabella, that all the blood in
her veins would smart as she suffered for his wife in her humiliation.

And he knew with a feeling of joy that Miss Renny was trapped. Just as
Miss Renny had managed to trap him into putting up with her obnoxious
presence by persistently brain-washing him with the myth of her indispensability, so Miss Renny herself was trapped in his flat for the night. She could
leave in the morning, but she had no choice but to remain in the flat for
the night, for Miss Renny had nowhere else to go. He was certain that she was
too nervously fussy and self-caring to dare to walk out in disgust into the
raining streets with her suitcase. He counted on the fact that she was far too

46

parsimonious to go off and find herself a room in a hotel.

He had always sensed that somewhere buried in the centre of Miss Renny's confident and overbearing personality, there was a sensitive little pocket of prudery and terror. And before Miss Renny left his flat he wanted to jab this spinsterish and shockable little area of Miss Renny's soul and make her suffer. He did not want her to leave until he had made her feel that she had been bruised and battered. This last night under his roof he hoped she would experience something far more upsetting than she had yet experienced in all her 'experience'.

The hatred that he felt for Miss Renny as he came swaying into the flat with the blonde girl was quite disproportionate to the harm she had actually done him. He longed to horrify and distress her, not so much because he wanted to revenge himself for all the unpleasant hours he had spent under the domination of her greedy, blackmailing personality, as for the fact that he could never forgive her because she had had such a peephole view of the collapse of his marriage. He felt that Miss Renny could never be punished enough because she had penetrated his privacy and watched with her uncaring and prying eye while the birth of his child turned to something that seemed far less like a birth than some long drawn out and painful death. Miss Renny had eaten her cakes and drunk her wine while his relationship with his wife deteriorated until he now felt certain that it was quite beyond repair. For he now found that he no longer wanted Arabella to recover. Having once longed for the return of her old self, it now seemed to him to be something so remote that he had become resigned to its loss and in no way wanted it. He could feel far more regret for his own lack of interest in the return of the old Arabella than he could regret her disappearance. Throughout so many lonely boring dinners with Miss Renny he had been kept afloat by his faith that his unpleasant and severed relationship with his wife was impermanent. As if to a raft, he had clung to his hope that their old flirtatious relationship would be restored unimpaired by her cure. But now he realised he no longer wanted Arabella cured or uncured. He found it impossible to imagine that he could ever revive any physical interest in her again. He wanted to get some doctor to put her in a hospital where he would no longer feel he had any responsibility for her. The prostrated dispirited creature who was lying there in her dirty bed in the flat seemed not only like someone who was dead to him — but like someone who had died before he was born.

'Is your wife away?' The blonde girl asked him as they came into the flat.

'I don't have a wife.'

'Well, you certainly didn't manage to keep her very long. I stuck mental pins into that girl when you married her. What a waste of all that green-eyed emotion. But then waste seems to be my middle name!'

He took the blonde girl into the store-room.

'You must be joking! Are you insane? You have this big flat. Is it some new subtle perversion that you find it exciting to sleep in the broom-cupboard?'

'It has a bed, hasn't it?'

The blonde girl looked at the rickety camp-bed with disgust.

'Did you force your beautiful bride to share this magnificent bed? I don't wonder that she didn't stay very long!'

'Shut up,' he said. 'Come over here.'

'Don't mawl me. What's the big hurry? We've got all night. Can't we have a drink first? Why are you being so rough? You didn't use to be rough. Marriage doesn't seem to have suited you. It's made you very peculiar. I've noticed that all evening. What on earth is the matter with you? Are you sex-starved or something?'

He wanted her to undress so that she would be naked when she met Miss Renny. She was starting to irritate him in the same way that in the past she had always irritated him. He found that the parting of her long peroxided hair was too low — annoyingly wrong, so that he wanted to seize her skull and shift it. When he got her to take off her sweater her skin looked too white, unhealthy, as if it were an unpleasant mixture of marble and rubber. He had always found her vulgar, over-compliant, and over-available, and he had never liked the way she was both martyred and critical in her over-compliant over-availability.

'It doesn't surprise me that Arabella has left you,' she said.

'Why is that?'

'You invented her. Women never like that. Arabella was such a brilliant actress . . . Arabella was so much cleverer and more charming than any other girl . . . I never thought she ever really wanted to marry you. I think she just liked to feel she had the power to make you want to marry her. Arabella was never in love with anything except her own elegant figure. I always felt there was something quite wrong with that girl. She had a peculiar stare in her big green eyes. I always thought she looked a bit psychotic.'

'Will you go next door and get us the bottle of Scotch which is on one of the shelves in the kitchen?'

48

He could hear that Miss Renny was stirring. She must have heard voices. She always prowled around in the night and made herself tea and snacks. He had always suspected that Miss Renny deliberately kept herself awake at night for fear of missing some explosive bedroom argument between Arabella and himself. But Miss Renny had been cheated of her arguments. In all her weeks of hopeful listening there had been nothing for her eager ear to pick up except a silence, the futureless silence of two hostile strangers both engrossed in totally different newspapers as they travelled in the same compartment in some train.

The blonde girl went off to get the whisky from the kitchen. As her naked, marble, rubber figure disappeared, his heart was pounding as he listened. Miss Renny was coming down the corridor. He could hear the shuffle of her bedroom slippers. And then he heard nothing. And then he heard what he had hoped to hear. Two screams. The scream of the blonde girl and the louder scream of Miss Renny.

And then suddenly the blonde girl was back in the storage-room. She was very angry, and her bad temper in conjunction with her nudity made her appear a little ludicrous.

'You are a bloody swine! Why didn't you tell me that there was someone else in this flat? Why on earth did you let me go roaming around in the nude? Do you realise that I just ran smack into your grandmother? You should have seen the poor creature's face! If she has a coronary tonight you deserve to be put on trial for murder.'

'That wasn't my grandmother. That was my mistress.'

'Don't try to be so amusing. I don't find what you did amusing. I find it pointless, and embarrassing for everyone, and really very cruel. But then I shouldn't be surprised by your cruelty. Ever since I've known you the way you have treated me has always been extremely cruel. It was certainly cruel the way you were too cowardly to tell me that you were besotted by the beautiful Arabella. I will never forgive you for that. If you had had the courage to tell me yourself I wouldn't have suffered so much. You think you are being so kind by acting in a cowardly weak way and then you do something which is really quite savage . . .'

'It seems a little late to rake up all that past stuff.'

'Oh, so it's all "past stuff" to you! If it's all "past stuff" why the hell did you bring me back here to sleep with you tonight?'

'Oddly enough, I needed you tonight. I needed you more tonight than I've ever needed you.'

Now that Miss Renny had seen her naked he wished that the blonde girl would leave. He suddenly found her intensity very tiring. She was frenziedly pulling back on all her clothes and she was trying to be as sexually provocative as possible while at the same time she appeared to be enjoying her own display of pique.

'Oh, so you needed me! Well, that's just wonderful! I'm afraid you are going to have to go on needing me. Your glamorous wife has the sense to walk out on you and then you find yourself forced to resort to second best. You never needed me tonight. But I know what you did need. You needed to reassure yourself that I was still infatuated with you. I imagine that your poor little ego must be feeling a little deflated right now and you needed me to pump it up like a bicycle tyre. Well, it's a bit late for that, lover boy. I see through you now . . .'

The blonde girl was speaking so loudly that he felt certain that Arabella must be listening to every word. He wondered if she would come out of her room. If she did he decided that he would introduce her to the blonde girl. Both of them seemed so unreal to him that he could feel not the faintest interest in their confrontation. He saw them both as two faded phantoms, and their meeting merely seemed like an eerie abstraction. Maybe they would condole with each other, maybe they would be vituperative, maybe they would be very formal and shake hands.

Miss Renny suddenly seemed to have more substance and reality than either of them. While the spit and spite of the blonde girl's tirade continued, he found that he couldn't stop thinking about Miss Renny. She would leave in the morning. He knew there was no doubt about that. And knowing that she was going, she suddenly seemed to dwindle. In his imagination he found that even her obesity appeared to be oddly diminished. The imminence of her departure seemed to strip Miss Renny of all her omnipotence and she was starting to shrivel away until she became nothing more than an unimportant old woman whose profession forced her to live always in the houses of strangers, and whose only future was her own retirement to some lonely drab cottage by the sea.

He was only too certain that he had succeeded in shocking her. She was being so quiet. She was being far too quiet. He suspected that she was now feeling far too frightened even to dare come out of her room. He knew that his behaviour this evening would make her feel that the whole flat was dangerously polluted, that all its poisons were even seeping into all the bottles she had so carefully sterilised for the baby. He knew that Miss Renny would never be able to sleep tonight. He could imagine her pacing in panic up and down her room feeling that she was trapped in a cage with rattle-snakes. He was only too certain that all night long her spinster's mind would be tormented by her own obscene imaginings.

And the more he thought about it, the more his successful shocking of Miss Renny seemed unnecessary. It had really solved so little. It had been a symbolic gesture. And now he felt that like so many symbolic gestures it had an in-built and symbolic futility.

The blonde girl was still abusing him. 'I don't know whether you realise it – but you are far less attractive than you were two years ago. You used to have a naïve little-boy quality. That's why women liked you. But something unpleasant has happened to you. You seem to have become even more hard and even more weak. I'm not sure that your sort of charm is the kind that ages very well. You may well be the kind of man who ends up lonely. Who is going to want a lot of little Lord Fauntleroy velvet on a man with thinning hair?'

The blonde girl's abuse distressed him very little for he knew that there had to be an end to it. The blonde girl was not taking care of the infant. He was in no way dependent on her. Eventually the blonde girl would leave. He felt that nothing was intolerable if it was possible to visualise some eventual end to it.

THE INTERVIEW

'You ask me if I liked the film we have just seen. No . . . No . . . I couldn't really say that I did.'

The painter's widow sat facing the journalist in the bar of a hotel. She was much taller than he was. The bones of her elbows were so sharp they looked like weapons. Her black clothes were crumpled and out of style as though they had just been dragged out of some children's dressing-up trunk which had been lying around for years in an attic.

'This film based on your late husband's life . . . Could you give me any reasons why you disliked it?'

'Did I ever say that I disliked the film? I do hope that you won't get too tricky and start misquoting me. Journalists can be so very ruthless. Can I ask you to be a little kind to me this evening? I have to tell you that I am feeling rather peculiar – that I am feeling almost faint. It was so very hot in that projection room – so airless. No . . . it seemed much worse than that – it seemed quite suffocating to me. When you invited me to come to this bar I didn't know that I would have to give an interview. Why did you never tell me that? I have nothing to say which could interest you. But you seem to be a very charming young man. Could we just drink and talk for a while and forget about the interview? It's a treat for me suddenly to be alone with a charming young man. I never go out you know. I don't think that you could imagine how rarely I ever go out.'

'I was wondering if you could give me a few of your reasons for disliking the film.'

'Disliking? Oh, that most inadequate word again! All the time they were showing me that film it never once occurred to me to try to judge it as though it was a Western. I was really only thinking how fortunate they were in the old days for they never had to go through anything like that. I was thinking that this was a new kind of torture.'

'Could you expand on that? Could you expand?'

'Well, in the old days at least they allowed you to lose your dead, to lose them so successfully you no longer felt them to be much of a loss. I'm sure that was very much better. But why are you looking so alarmed? Am I making no sense? Am I being too rhetorical and affected? I'm afraid it's because I so rarely go out. If you are always alone you start to lose the knack of talking normally to other people. But I'm afraid that I can't really blame it all on loneliness. My husband often used to say that whenever I felt anything very strongly, I always became flowery, and embarrassing, and tended to overstate. He said that was why I would never be able to paint. He was right of course, and I knew it. I gave up painting as you may know, although I had quite a little reputation in my day.'

'May I quote you as saying that your husband forced you to give up painting?'

'You are becoming tediously tricky again. He was certainly never frightened of my competition, if that's what you are getting at. It was something a little more intricate than that. Can you just tell me how two people can expect to live together for more than a week if both of them want to paint? Maybe you can have a couple both doing the same thing in other arts. Two musicians might possibly be a little noisy. But all the paraphernalia of painting. Oh dear! And then two separate studios – his and hers. Surely that becomes more than faintly ridiculous. And can you imagine two sets of crippling bills from the framer and a couple squabbling because both of them want to grab the north light?'

'Could you talk a little more about the film?'

'Oh, I was so afraid that you would want me to do that! I have been rambling. I can see by your face that already you are starting to find me impossibly tiresome. But it's curious that while I was watching that film I was wondering if my tiresomeness was not one of the qualities that my late husband most valued in me. It made it possible for him to use me as a lightning-conductor for the dislike that he tended to arouse so easily in so many people. If I was present he could always trust me to deflect all the zig-zags of their hate away from himself.'

'That sounds interesting. Will you please go on?'

'Why do you keep on speaking to me with such exaggerated politeness, young man? I find your professional soft-spokenness very disturbing. It makes me feel that I must be nearer to the end than I care to face. It's as though you were laying down straw to muffle the sound of carriage wheels outside my house. You don't need to use so much courtesy to extract a lot of indiscreet prattle for your copy. Can't you just drop all your dreary deference and get me another drink?'

The journalist watched uneasily as her spiky arm reached out and sucked her new whisky under the curtain of black fish-net veiling which draped down from her enormous hat. The journalist had never seen such a hat.

'You want me to get back to that obnoxious film . . . Well, all the time I was sitting there in the dark I was thinking that tapes and reel can sometimes be rather a violation – particularly tapes. It was hearing his voice that I found the worst. Oh I do think that they were lucky in the old days! There were portraits and drawings then, of course, but they can have none of that awful mirage liveliness.'

'Are you trying to say that this film distressed you because it reminded you of your husband?'

'I never once tried to say that it reminded me of my husband. Oh, I'm so sorry! Oh, please excuse me! I didn't mean to snap at you. It's just that although you may find me a befuddled old woman, you may notice that I tend to be rather careful when it comes to using words. To be reminded of some-one – surely they have to be absent. Then, of course, any trivia can be a reminder, a photograph, an ash-tray, or a sock. But he wasn't absent this after-noon. It was precisely that which I found so unsettling. There he was . . . He was speaking – he was moving – he was smiling. He was present. But I don't think that I ever felt before that he was quite so absent. Why do you think I am sitting here with you in this odious bar? You have your wonderful white teeth and your shy grin. You have very strong hands – I always notice hands. You have eyes as cold as tiny frozen French peas. But one forgets that as soon as you give your corrupt little disarming grin. And then you have that nice tufty hair. But do you really think that I like you so much? Do you think that I long to give an interview? Tonight I just don't feel that I want to be alone. He looked so healthy and he looked so lively, and even when I was staring at the great polished studs on his coffin, I don't think that I ever felt that he was quite so dead.'

'Is there anything I can do? Would you like to move nearer to a window? Would you feel better if you had more air?'

'I must apologise for my seizure of swaying and shaking. I assume that you find all my black veiling absurd. I wonder if you are glad now that it makes it difficult for you to tell if I am laughing or crying? But why do you make me feel that I am wasting your time? You are so anxious to continue – you are relentless . . . And yet you are really very kind to me. My little breakdown has made you so nervous that I see you have suddenly ordered me a full bottle of whisky. You don't need to charge it up on your expense account you know. I can pay for my own drinks. I can't do much any more. Maybe that's why I so like to pay.'

'Are you sure that you feel well enough to go on? . . . Would you say that this film will give the public a fair picture of your husband?'

'A fair picture! You must excuse me for laughing! What a jackass they made him seem. But somehow that didn't really surprise me.'

'A jackass?'

'Oh, yes. How very awful they made him seem — so sort of fatuous, and famous.'

'Was there anything in the way that your husband was presented which you found specifically objectionable?'

'Why are you staring so suspiciously at my fingers? Do you find it intriguing that they tinkle like tambourines when I move them, they are wearing so many rings? But to get back . . . Oh I suppose that I was bound to be most depressed by all that frightful smiling. Now I concede that he must have smiled occasionally. How else could they have got hold of so much film of him grinning like some cartoon cat? But I must say that one can sometimes be quite grateful that one's memory is so feeble. For although I may remember various unsavoury things about him, I still thank God that despite this film, I will never, ever, remember him as a man who was always smiling. This afternoon on the screen, it was really amazing! If he primed a canvas in his studio — there he was beaming. Even if he took a walk alone by the sea he still seemed to be chortling. Oh, it was really horrifying to see him! Whether he was chatting with some celebrity, or receiving some honour, or just cracking his egg for breakfast, it was like an affliction the way that he seemed so unable to ever stop smiling. You know sometimes I felt like shouting at him from my seat, but I thought it might be a little disturbing for the director and all those distributors.'

'Could you tell me what you would like to have shouted?'

'Oh, I don't know. Just something silly, like children shout. What's so funny, Mr Bunny?'

'Apart from his smiling, was there anything else that troubled you in the film?'

'Oh, yes. I was quite troubled by the way that he seemed to have learned so little.'

'Could you make yourself a little clearer?'

'If someone comes back to pay you an afternoon visit from the dead somehow one expects that they will have learned something — maybe even have been a little changed by their experiences. But he seemed to know rather less than the last time that I saw him. It was as though he was too pleased with himself, and too busy smiling to have taken in anything at all. Maybe it was because they kept showing so much film of him as a young man. All the same, I couldn't help finding him rather a disappointing Lazarus.'

'I think you will agree that your late husband was considered to be a notoriously egocentric and difficult character. As his wife, no doubt you suffered more than anyone from what might politely be called his "artistic temperament". Is it possible that you disliked the film, not for any of the reasons you have given me, but because you resented the fact that it presents what might seem to you to be such a whitewashed, half-picture of the man?'

'He was incontinent at the end. Did you know that?'

'What has that to do with my question?'

'I was just wondering if you would now like to suggest that I disliked the film because it gave no close-ups of his incontinence.'

If she had won a round there was no one listening to keep her score.

'It has sometimes been said that in your relationship to your late husband, you were always more of a mother to him than a wife. Would you say that was true?'

'Oh, I know that people always like to say a lot of boring simplistic things like that. No, I would almost certainly never say that I was ever his mother for the very obvious reason that he always *had* a mother. Admittedly she was a disapproving old prune of a woman and it always upset and embarrassed him whenever she came to see him. But there she was. And she outlived him, and the fact is that he *always* had her. If he had any mother apart from his real one, I would say that in his last years it was most probably only alcohol. Certainly that was the only thing which could get him up and dressed in the morning and help him to go toddling and tottering from A to B. It was the only thing which could soothe away a few of his aches and anxieties and get him to sleep at night . . . What more can you expect from any mother?'

'Did your husband continue to paint when he was under the influence of what you call this "mother"?'

'Oh, yes. He always went on painting spasmodically. It didn't matter. I never let him release any of the work that he did in that last period. Whenever he finished a canvas, I usually went into his studio a little later and ripped it to pieces with a razor. There's always a certain pleasure in getting rid of rubbish. I suppose that's why housewives enjoy spring cleaning.'

'Was your husband grateful for your solicitude – your spring-cleaning?'

'Oh, it would make him snarl and smash things, of course, and sometimes it would make him cry, but I never worried about that too much.'

'I'm quite sure you didn't!'

'You are so shocked my pure young man! But your piety is so platitudinous – the piety of the Press. Now can you imagine a man who has had his hands cut off? How would you hope for him to be treated by anyone close to him? Surely in so far as possible they should try to be his lost hands. Well, if a man loses his judgment . . .'

'When you took it upon yourself to judge your husband's work did it ever occur to you that other critics might consider your destruction of these paintings to be an act of criminal irresponsibility?'

'Naturally I knew I was destroying work which certain people would consider valuable. Oh, I could have let the dealers into his studio of course. They would have only too quickly pronged up all his litter like gardeners cleaning up a public park. But you must remember that even when he became very little more than one big hiccup of a man, he still went on being that curious insect-like creature, the paranoid. He could walk blind, but his antennae were out in front, always quivering and ever-ready to detect the insult. Do you think that he wouldn't have sensed that they were all stripping him, although they found it time-wasting even to look at his work? Who bothers to examine the designs on pieces of paper if those pieces come from the mint? Under such circumstances, what use would a few more soulless sales have been to someone who was already rather like a steaming punch-bowl of mixed alcohol, all the fuss of his own fame had made him feel so fraudulent?'

'Your protective concern for your late husband's feelings all sounds immensely touching, but is it true that you now own the world's largest private collection of his paintings?'

'Maybe I do. How would I know? I think that people are often shocked on the rare occasions that they come to my home, because I have never bothered to hang a single canvas. They are all lying about unframed and dusty, just stacked against the walls, exactly as they used to be when they were in his studio. My husband always said that he found it repulsive for a painter to hang his own work. He always had a horror of imposing on his guests and friends – of forcing them to comment – worst of all to praise. He said there were few things as depressing as a house which made you feel that some seedy gallery was having a one-man show.'

'But your husband disliked the idea of displaying his *own* work. May I ask you why you take this peculiar pride in refusing to hang work which is not *your* work?'

'His work *is* my work.'

'Your collection has now become immensely valuable?'

'Very possibly. I've certainly never troubled to have it valued. I've kept all his clothes, you know. I never look at them — I never display them. I found most of them pretty shabby when he was alive. I certainly don't like them any better now. But somehow I don't get rid of them. It's exactly the same with the paintings.'

'Naturally. Naturally. I know that you pretend to be completely disinterested in the value of your collection, but you have admitted to me that you destroyed a lot of your husband's work — work which for all anyone knows may have included many masterpieces. Could it be that you were simply frightened that he might overflood his market? Were you really only protecting your own future investments?'

'Masterpieces! Masterpieces! Oh, how you love the patter of your own mindless jargon, my little journalist! What on earth can the very word masterpiece mean to you? Anything that's one big fat masterpiece of money. Now allow *me* to ask you a question. Why are you sitting there writing down my whisky-soaked words? You have no possible interest in me — and just as little in him. To you we are both simply like the cardboard wrappers on some best-selling soapflake. Your only concern with us is our closeness to a successful commercial product?'

'May I compliment you? You are very quick to avoid answering the awkward question.'

'Oh, yes . . . My husband always used to say that I was like the punchballs that boxers use for practice. They look as though they are pinioned there just waiting to take a slam, but they turn out to have just that little bit more mobility than you think and sometimes they can dodge and spin on their springs and can leave you punching at air.'

'You are all dressed up in your black. It is obvious that you like to meet the world as the bereaved widow. Yet whenever you mention your husband's name your tone is always curiously malicious and scathing. Will I meet with your famous evasiveness if I ask you if you can claim that during his lifetime you and he were ever very close?'

'How odd it is to be sitting here in this unpleasant hotel with the muzac soothing me like a lullaby, while I allow a stranger to pester me with painful and impertinent questions. Oh, we were close all right . . . but only in the sense that the criminal is close to his accomplice. I think that it was always a relief to him to have someone with whom he felt he could share his guilt. But then there was an uglier side. There was also so much distrust. Today when I saw him again on the screen I was wondering if it was really always only fear which made him feel that he had to stay close to me – if it was as though I knew too much, and he was convinced that he had to pay me off, for unless I was per-petually placated he might find himself exposed. You couldn't possibly under-stand a guilt like his, it was like a perforated ulcer leaking blood into his intestines. You would find his crime so pathetically unimportant. And yet in a sense he died to atone for the fact that at its best, his work was so deeply second-rate . . .'

Like someone whose eyes have become accustomed to the dark the journalist found that he was starting to be able to see through the murky clouds of her veiling. He could make out eyes so sunken and black they looked like craters, corrugated cheeks which were flaked and mealy with face-powder, a collapsed mouth which was scarlet, greasy, and painted.

'And yet he was always so frightened of death. It's funny, I really never have been.'

The journalist nodded, for as he stared at her it seemed to him that death had already made some gigantic attack on her and failed. Now he saw it as very unlikely that it would find the energy quickly to try again. All the flesh and fluids of her body appeared to have been already carried off. It was as though there was nothing left to her which could ever become dried up or destroyed. As she sat there, he felt she was embalmed, safely pickled and preserved for eternity inside her crusty parchment skin. When she repeated that she had never had any fear of death he grunted quite sympathetically, as though for the first time he felt that what she said was true.

'You seem to be a very forceful and ambitious woman. As a failed painter yourself, it cannot have been very easy for you to live in the shadow of your husband's success. Would you admit that some old feeling of rivalry may be operating when you get so much obvious pleasure from denigrating his achieve-ment?'

'What can you possibly know of his achievement? Oh, how I wish you would stop using all those vacuous newspaper words! I very much doubt that you had even heard his name before you were sent out today on your assignment.

And now I find it really rather comical — if I say that his work was second-rate you give a jump! And what makes you dare to assume that I say it disparagingly? Does it never occur to you that, as a failed painter myself, I might consider that in the scale of things, the second-rate painter ranks really rather high?'

'Your open admiration for his second-rateness must have always been a great comfort and encouragement to your husband in his lifetime!'

'Oh, yes . . . But you don't need to give your sarcastic little laugh. In some perverse way I most certainly think it was. You see, when he became so fashionable, it was as though he felt publicly branded with some kind of total worthlessness. He was oddly honourable, though that side of him never came through in the film. He was also intelligent, though often his intelligence could only act as an irritant to plague him. He always feared that fashion was like those modern garbage disposal units which can gobble up anything — or rather anything that's small enough — potato peelings, mushy tea-leaves, any old rotten bones. I always tried to make him remember that the same machine can also suck down small flowers. But I'm afraid that all he cared was that once it had pulverised and reduced everything to the same swilly consistency — it usually sank it deep in the ground.'

'Now your husband may have been as troubled by his success as you like to claim, but I find it hard to believe that you yourself found it all that disagreeable. This is impertinent — but from the way that you speak of him — I wonder why you stayed with him. It's as though all you ever felt for him was some kind of lofty contempt and hate.'

'Hate? Hate? . . . Oh I certainly tried to make him die, if that's what you mean. I smuggled him so many bottles of whisky into the hospital, and when his doctors discovered they treated me exactly as though I was a murderess. He was just one big tissue of needles and plastic tubes at that point — and more than all the pain, I knew that he minded the indignity. His great doctors squeezed him out about four extra months by taking so much cosseting care of his liver which was a sinking ship of an organ if ever there was one. But maybe they were right. I often think about that. When I visited him just towards the end, he told me that once you knew that that was it . . . then it wasn't quite so bad. He said that your whole time-sense changed and that the most trivial experience seemed valuable and in some new and magical way, total. He claimed that he could just lie and watch a fly buzzing across his room and get as much out of it as he once had from visiting a new country. Of course, I never believed him for one second — he was much too cowardly for there to be any

60

chance that what he was saying was true. He was always someone who made you feel that if you were to cut open his brain, you would find it all pitted and eaten up with some sort of dreadful dry-rot of morbid fears. Under the circumstances, how could one believe that someone like that could get all that much comfort from watching the buzzing of some dismal fly? But still — he claimed that he could — so one assumes that he was trying to spare someone. He was never in the very slightest bit unselfish — so one feels it was unlikely that he was trying to spare me . . . Did you know that the ancient Turks had a favourite torture? They used to leave their prisoners lying all day tied to planks which were nailed so that they jutted out over the sides of precipices. In the evening, the planks would be sawn away, but meanwhile, the victims were given a lot of time to examine every needle point of rock that lay down below in the ravine where they knew they would soon be hurtling. His great doctors kept him on a very similar plank in that hospital, I think. But that's old stuff and nothing can be done about it now. I can see that you are looking quite glazed with boredom. You feel that you can't use a word of this for your interview. Ask me more questions young man. It amuses me to see you taking such a professional pride in all your provocative questions. I really rather love your ludicrous little idea that an experienced approach is needed to draw me out. If only you knew . . . if only you knew . . . After seeing that film today, I'm afraid that no very expert handling is needed to make me talk. I can promise you, my dear young man, that if I was at home alone tonight, I would be talking to the mirror . . . I wonder if you know anything about budgerigars. They are such very silly birds. They start to pine if they find themselves alone in a cage, but if you give them a mirror, they perch themselves in front of it and start to preen themselves and chirp. You see, when they see their own reflection, they think they have a mate. Now I don't know if you've realised — I'm sure you think that you are very sophisticated, and to me you seem quite naïve — but all the time you've been questioning me I've been wondering whether I should take you back with me to my house when it gets late. I was thinking that if I was to go on talking, and talking to you all night — just using you as a mirror — you never know, . . . but eventually I might even start to think you were my mate.

'Now you shouldn't look so petrified! Your face has gone quite puce and I thought I saw you shudder. If you feel like shuddering — don't you think it's wrong to let me see? I might still have a little vanity left you know — I was once such a striking and sought-after woman. I must say it's a disappointment to discover that you are so deeply prudish and conventional. As you've

61

pecked me with so many — may I be permitted to ask you a question? Can you tell me one good reason why tonight I should not be allowed to think of you as a mate? You are obviously very frightened of old women — but that is so very childish. I will have to teach you that old age is not really like a germ which you might catch if you get too close to it. If I take you home with me, I will also have to make the whole thing worthwhile for you — I know that. I've always been oddly shrewd though I seem so scattered. I will show you all his "masterpieces" as you like to call them. Now how could an art-connoisseur like yourself resist such a rare and intense experience? In the morning when you leave me, I may very well allow you to cart away a great stack of them with you in a wheelbarrow. Ah now! I'm afraid that that's the first thing I've said to you which you have found genuinely interesting! . . . Now I've made you jump because you wonder if I'm sane — and if insane, serious. Well, when I look at you with your white teeth, and your chic little summer suit and your greedy weasel eyes, I feel quite serious. You are so very knowing and so completely ignorant. The shoddiness of your values actually seems to shine out of every pore of your skin like phosphorus. Oh, I certainly think that you deserve to have them. At least you would have the good sense to throw them all immediately on to the market like firewood. You would have none of my procrastinating apathy. You are a journalist after all and more than anyone you ought to know the life-span of publicity. You ought to know how long it's possible for his prices to continue their crazy pumped-up pirouette.'

'May we please go on with the interview? I soon have another appointment.'

'You have another appointment — and you are now obviously starting to regret it. You are such a little opportunist — and you are aware that this might be rather a special opportunity. But now I'm getting tired of teasing you. I'm afraid that I'm too passive to be nearly as predatory as I've been pretending. I'm still glad that I managed to disturb and embarrass you. I feel that I deserved to do that. Today I was forced to sit through a film which made me feel that my whole past was being thrown back at me all curiously curdled and distorted — rather like food that comes back as vomit. And then immediately after that I was asked to answer what to you may seem to be a lot of standard, set-piece questions. But how will you ever know or care what a hive of disturbing feelings those questions may have stirred up in me?'

'I'm very sorry that you have found this interview so painful. I can assure you that I am every bit as anxious to terminate it as you are. There are just one or two questions I would like to ask before I leave you — naturally you are under no obligation to answer me. You strike me as being a woman with a rather highly developed sense of your own importance. Did you feel that this film distorted the facts when it presented you as quite a minor character while your husband was made to play so very much the star? Did you find it in bad taste that they showed him in so many reels in the company of Marina Casatti?'

'I find your first question too facetious to be worth answering – but Marina . . . I think that seeing Marina again was perhaps the only thing in that vulgar little film that I did like. She was quite important for a while you know. I think that they had a perfect right to show her. At the time he sometimes claimed that I wouldn't release him. He said to me once that I had the mind of a queen and the soul of a peasant – and that a peasant never likes to let go of a good property. I found that curious because I was always convinced that it was the other way round. I never felt for a moment that he ever wanted to stop clinging on to my passivity. Passivity – even a rather disgruntled and critical passivity – can be quite solid you know. It can be like a wall, and you can twine yourself on to it like a strand of dusty ivy, and it takes a certain time before you start to loosen all the bricks. But enough of that – let me talk about Marina. I used to hate her so much and now it all seems so long ago. I'm sure that you would find it primitive and peasant-like the way I used to hate her. I remember that I once wrote her name on a large wooden spoon – the kind that you use to stir puddings. I intended to take the spoon up to the local cemetery and to stick it in some newly dug grave. I had heard that you could bring misfortune to someone that way – and I so wanted something quite appalling to happen to Marina. But just as I set off, it started to rain and then my usual inertia set in, and I kept thinking how damp and depressing it was going to be in the cemetery. I thought how embarrassing it would be if I was caught kneeling beside a frothed-up grave by some unctuous little choir-boy or church-functionary. I was frightened I might end up on some mortifying police charge for the violation of sacred property. Today, when I saw Marina showing-off on the screen, I was glad that I never went near any graveyard with my spoon. She was killed in a car crash as you may know. You may find it ridiculous, but if I'd done what I wanted to then, I'm certain I would always have felt somehow superstitiously responsible. And sitting there this afternoon in that smoky projection room all that I wondered was how I could have ever thought for one moment that Marina could get much more out of him than I could. Do you think two people can ever get very different water from the same old polluted well? And what a joyless companion he was at his best – his feeling of failure seemed to be always strapped to his back like a knapsack!

63

It was often also rather like being with some kind of ruthless and canny sleuth. He always seemed to be trying to track down something valuable which he seemed to feel had been stolen from him. He spied on everyone – suspected everyone. Oh, he was so sly! He made everyone feel that he was planning to sneak into their room to ransack their baggage. And then what a morose and unshaven lover – as a performer just about as soft and green as asparagus! But I can see that I am making you very uneasy when I talk like this. I admit that I may be sprouting a few sour grapes because of Marina. Yet seeing her again today I really felt quite sorry that she now only exists as a breasty image on celluloid. You have been really quite patient with me – and we all know you have those nice white teeth – and it may seem rather perverse to you – but tonight I would rather be drinking here with Marina, than interviewing here with you.'

'I must be going. Thank you for giving me your valuable time.'

'I find it hard to believe that you are really leaving. Journalists are scavengers and they rarely like to leave while there's still a shred of flesh sticking to the carcase. And I would like to know when you are going to send me what you have written about me. I'm convinced that I'm going to like it – that I may feel forced to memorise every word like a poem. One always delights to find oneself described in clichés. It's like being so well wrapped up in thick wads of cotton-wool padding that one becomes invisible. Now what can be more comforting? And then it's so elating to know that even if one's quite badly shaken one can suffer very little real damage . . . But do I see you gathering up all your papers and tucking them away in your ugly brown attaché case? That makes me feel panicky. Oh, please don't leave me! Can I beg you on my knees just to stay and talk a little longer? I would have so liked to ask you to dine with me – but I'm afraid that I've said something to offend you. You see I know that I should never have sat through that film today. I fear that film can be a little too factual – and its effects can be rather fatal. One should only ever be linked to the past through one's memory. Luckily memory is the most miserable, and unreliable, old muscle. I'm sure that a young man like you must laugh at people of my age because they tend to live too much in the past, but when all the hills in front of you start to seem to be dipping down into the most grey and unmentionable valleys – I can assure you that the very last thing you will want to see is a film which makes you realise that no past exists for you which is in any way very livable to live in. Why on earth do you think that I'm over-staying now in all this sordid plush? Only because all those flash-backs that I've seen today have made me feel so homeless . . . I'm afraid that it has to be rather depressing to be reminded that no one can live very comfortably in a past which they never found remotely pleasant while it was still a present – and which they wasted by always sitting about passively and pointlessly, waiting for some less painful future.'

'Yes . . . Yes . . . I think everything valuable has already been covered. A friend of mine has arrived. I would now like to say goodnight.'

'How can you be so cruel as to jump up impatiently and leave me here alone? You should tell me where I am – why the deck seems so slippery and keeps sloping away in the storm. And who is she now? May I ask why she suddenly seems to be joining you? I have to tell you that I find her arrival most unwelcome. She looks rather insipid to me with her mousey-pale curls – a little too like some damp slightly soiled, powder puff. All my life I've known such girls – they balance so badly on their high-heel shoes. All my life I've tried to avoid such girls. And then I find her very rude. How dare she come from nowhere to interrupt us? I wish that she wouldn't stutter and try to apologise. She has stopped the band just when the wall-flower thought she was finally going to be able to take to the floor. How can her bogus apologies make amends for that? She is obviously still planning to take you away from me. Well . . . you are a coarse-surfaced and hard thing, just something suitable to strike matches on. But what makes her think that I've quite finished with you? Oh now . . . I see by her face I've frightened her. I'm afraid that was inevitable. Tonight I feel that I might be frightened if I met myself. It would be like meeting some deranged and decapitated ghost that has just discovered it has spent several decades haunting the wrong corridor. But would you please mind taking your hand off my shoulder young man. I dislike being steadied as though I was a toppling milk bottle. Now I admit that you and your powder-puff girl friend seem to be suddenly hanging down from the ceiling. You are dangling now in the distance – two very dim chandeliers. But at such moments some unwanted jab of sobriety always seems to come pricking through the novocaine. And one likes to be granted the favour of being allowed to make one's exit unaided.'

'Goodnight. Goodnight. If you go through that door on the left I'm sure you will pick up a cab in the street.'

'But my hat is tipping over my eye. I must look much more jaunty than I feel. There's still no need for you both to hustle me out. I only long to go back home now. I could ask you to come back and dine with me – but tonight I suddenly feel that I would rather be alone with my monkeys. It's curious, but I always seem to have kept monkeys – I've always been very attached to them – they have amused me more than most things. I've always been fascinated by

E

all their chattering, and their somersaults, and their dirty ways. I love to dress
them up in funny suits and give them tea-parties with tiny pots, and cups and
cakes. Sometimes I give them paper and strap brushes to their wrists and watch
them paint. Once in a while they will do something which is not entirely
uninteresting . . . But naturally that's just chance. Most of the time I'm afraid
that they just produce a predictable monkey mess. But why should one care
about that? It's still rather insane the way I'm devoted to them. I'll often sit
up all night with them when they get chills, and I'll hold them wrapped in
warm blankets, and I'll sip them little spoonfuls of aspirin in syrup. But then
all of a sudden some evening when I'm all alone with them – I start to get the
most scary and horrifying feeling that the whole lot of them are dying. I go
rushing over to their cages because I keep wondering if anyone has fed them.
I am almost certain that they are all starving and it makes me very angry, and
I want to blame someone – but somehow I find that I can't quite remember who
it is that I ought to be blaming. And it's strange – but I still don't feed them
myself, and I don't give them any water. Instead I draw up my chair, and I sit
myself down beside them and I just watch them lying there in their sawdust,
all limp, and sad, and panting. And I find that the longer I watch them, the
more I suspect that nothing is ever going to save them, and this makes me
very agitated. "What's the matter with you?" I often even shout at them aloud,
I feel so frantic – and naturally they never answer me. "Just tell me what's
the matter with you." I scream at them and I rattle the bars of their cages. And
then it's suddenly always quite a shock to realise that the reason why I have
such a strong feeling that nothing can ever save them – is that I really care
so very little if they are saved or not. For although they've served their purpose, and screeched, and clowned, and distracted me – yet despite all their
antics – they've never been quite what I want.'

The old woman started slowly shuffling out of the bar with her skirts trailing down limply over her pair of black, button-up boots. Suddenly she turned
and saw that the journalist was whispering to his friend.

'Couldn't you wait until I'm out of earshot? Your girl-friend likes me better
than you do. But then she has never tried to winkle-pin my character. You
find me a sinister old saddle-sore. She thinks that you still ought to see me
home – that you've made me dangerously drunk – I look so frail – and she
fears it's raining. I'm afraid I have to say that she lacks charisma – but
she has a little charity. I should be grateful . . . But I find her sympathy rather
like a fur-coat offered to one on a scorching day. I've often talked too much
about my monkeys – and found my own way home alone.'

HOW YOU LOVE OUR LADY

Father Callahan must be dead now – 'resting' – as he always liked to call it somewhere in the mud of his own churchyard. Maybe he is even still alive – maybe senile – and living in some cottage with a housekeeper. 'O songless bird far sweeter than the rose. And virgin as the Parish Priest. God knows!' They all quoted then. Sometimes they used to quote and counter-quote all through the night. I so loved to listen to them, sitting next to Father Callahan in the wonderful light of my mother's candles. They used to come to my mother's grey Georgian house from Dublin – some of them even came from further. My mother loved poets, painters and talkers. She said she could only bear to be surrounded by 'free-spirits'. She was always speaking about her love for Art and Nature, and sometimes she said that she thought that life should be one long search for the beautiful. My mother never made me go to bed. She said that she detested the tyranny of the clock and that all those who bowed to it were the poor trapped prisoners of the temporal. Often in the mornings when I walked up to my convent through those grey, rock roads bordered by hawthorns, I felt so weightless and really weird from lack of sleep that it seemed to me that there was very little to stop me from floating up to the great white melancholy morning sky, and becoming part of it. And I would feel that I could understand why my mother often started repeating, when she was drinking in the evenings, that she thought that Life and Death were really the same – and both were beautiful.

I never liked my convent. Even Father Callahan could never really persuade me to like those nuns with their long, cold corridors punctuated by tormented, bleeding plaster Christs. Those nuns with their child-like skins, their canes and their crucifixes. I found the other convent girls so brutal, crude and frightening. They made the new girls hang their breasts over a towel-rail and then pricked them with safety-pins. Any girl who screamed they pricked much harder right on her nipples. I used to be so modest then – I remember that I cried while still only waiting for my turn, finding the mortification of being forced

67

to stand half-naked in front of other girls almost as painful as the pricking. And long before they had drawn a drop of blood from me, I fainted. The Sisters were so cold, so fiercely disapproving, when I came to with ice-packs on my head in the sick-bay. They asked nothing – but I sensed that they could guess what had happened to me, and that like their own girls, they could feel only contempt for someone so frail – someone so completely lacking in the great qualities : courage, fortitude, self-sacrifice.

I learnt very little in my convent. I saw all my days as lost nights, and dawn only ever seemed to come to me when I was sitting after midnight, talking to Father Callahan in front of the heaped peat fires of my mother's drawing-room. I learnt only poetry to please my mother. Now I have forgotten almost all that I once knew. Who would want to listen to it now? My husband George slumped in his zombie stupor in front of the TV in our New York apartment? The elevator man? My coloured maid? It is strange but I still remember certain lines. 'A well dark-gleaming and of most translucent wave – images all the woven boughs above. And each depending leaf and every speck of azure sky . . .' My voice must have sounded so pure then. My mother would wipe her eyes when she heard it. She was always so proud of me when she saw me standing there reciting in my pretty white lace dress in the candle-light. In the evening when all her friends were there she would seem to feel a special warmth towards me and it would make her smile with delight if any of them said that I was like her. When we were alone together in the daytime I often felt a constraint, a nagging feeling of inadequacy as if I was perpetually failing her. Sometimes she made me feel like an egg that has been handpainted for Easter – an ordinary breakfast egg which shouldn't be fingered too much because all its gay dye can just come smudging off on the hand and then all its drab patches of everyday shell start to show. I knew that I had an underlay of drabness which distressed my mother far more than my occasional displays of insolence and disobedience. Whenever in her opinion I became commonplace she made it very clear that she only longed to get away from me, as if my dullness was like a disease that might contaminate her if she was too closely exposed to it. 'There is only one great crime', she would warn me. Her eyes would look almost blind as she spoke, as if they were filmed over with the glaucoma-like glaze of her own intensity. 'You can do what you like in this world. But you must always remember, Theresa, that the only great crime is to allow the humdrum to seep into your soul . . .' When she was in that kind of mood she nearly always started to talk about elms. She often said that you could get more education from just looking at trees and water than you could from wasting your days sitting on a hard bench in some nun-ridden soulless school. And then I would feel puzzled why she thought it necessary to send me to the convent. In any case elms were an obsession with her and she said they were the great tutors. 'Have you ever seen the way that an elm dies, Theresa? An elm doesn't die like other trees, you know. An elm dies from the inside. An elm dies in secret. You should always remember to be careful when you walk underneath elms for they can be dangerous. Elms are the only trees which give you no warning signs of their own decay. They can just come toppling down with a fearful crash while all their branches still look glorious and intact and all their leaves are still in bud. Once they are on the ground it can be quite frightening to see what has happened inside their trunks. Once they are dead you can see how the rot has eaten into them so hideously that they are completely hollow. People who allow themselves to become trivial and humdrum are like blighted elms. Eventually they are destroyed by being so filled with their own hollowness . . .' The more she would speak about dying elms, the more I would start to feel like one. Every thought that came into my head seemed like a threatening rot, it seemed to be so dull and dim and ordinary. Sometimes I feared that my mother had an X-ray power by which she could detect the banality of my unpromising thoughts and I pined to swallow some magic pill which would prevent me from ever boring her.

'You have misnamed your daughter,' my mother's friends would tell her after they had listened to me reciting in the evenings. 'The child is no Theresa. She is a Deirdre. Just look at that face! And the girl is ready for her Naisi — but now all our Deirdres are doomed to be guarded by nuns who are far fiercer and more deadly than any jealous old King Concubar!' — 'That child is not human,' they would keep repeating. 'She is one of the Sidhe!' The Sidhe — the enchanted spirit race of ancient Ireland. 'God fuck you!' they shouted at my mother, 'you are repeating the tragedy of the country. You give birth to a Sighoge — and you allow its lovely spirit to be mutilated in a bleeding convent!' They would lift up their glasses in a toast to me and then tip their wines and whiskys on to my mother's carpet. They smashed their glasses down on the floor and ground them to a sugary powder with their heels. They shouted things like 'Long live the Fenian men!' and 'Up the I.R.A.!' My mother would laugh and go to play her piano. Father Callahan would take my hand. I would feel his palms which were as cool, smooth and unused as those of a young child. He always took my hand when they started to blaspheme. Often when the wine was on them they would hurl blasphemies back and forth across the room like delinquents throwing stones. I was often frightened that

69

some dreadful flaming retribution would strike and smash the whole house. But then when Father Callahan took my hand I felt comforted, thinking that his very presence under our roof must act as some kind of talisman with the power to ward off the scourge of the Divine Anger. 'Never be disturbed by blasphemy,' he would whisper to me. 'Blasphemy is only the lining of the coat of Belief. Blasphemy is only the lining turned inside out.'

He must have been a very young man then, Father Callahan. It is hard for me even now to realise it. At the time he seemed like the bleak, beautiful hills that I could see from my mother's window, even older and sadder than Christianity. He drank, Father Callahan. This always rather surprised me. He drank solemnly, treating his wine as though it was a sacrament. And his drinking seemed to increase not only his sadness, but also his sobriety. My mother always served special vintage whiskys and brandies and very good French wines. She said that she could only tolerate the 'excellent' – that a true love of quality was a 'Life Caring'. She collected old blue Waterford glass and had very good plates on her dresser. She wore only beautiful laces and wine-coloured velvets. She said that she had to live beside water, that her blood came from the sea, and she claimed as an ancestor some fierce Spanish sailor who had been smashed up on the Galway rocks from the Armada. Outside her house a waterfall crashed through the night. Everyone had to shout in her drawing-room. They shouted against the cascade of water that fermented and foamed like angry beer as it hit the rocks. They shouted against the crash of my mother's piano. My mother always played very loud. She knew so many songs. All the new English songs, and the laments of the old Gaels. Her voice could sound as thunderous as any man's, and while she played and sang, her face flushed scarlet, her huge eyes flashed and rolled in her head, her great breasts heaved up and down so violently that they seemed about to break through her wonderful velvet dresses, and her long hair streamed down over her shoulders, ink-black from perspiration. Often as the night went on she seemed enchanted, almost demented by her own music. And frequently by the time that morning started to break on the hills it seemed as though her piano was really playing her – and she was only its exhausted instrument. And many times when she stopped her playing, she would fall like a stone to the ground.

'Your mother is a nymph!' Father Callahan once said to me. 'She is surely the very same nymph that sucked Finn down into the waters. It is no wonder that he stayed so long down there that his hair had turned white by the time that he came up again!' I think he knew how much it always pleased her when

70

anyone said rather exaggerated and high-flown things like that.

I wonder if I ever really properly understood the way that Father Callahan loved my mother. I always felt that his love for her was very different from the love of all the poets and drinkers and talkers who came every night to her drawing-room and so often ended up in the 'Doss-House' as they called her spare room where rows of mattresses were always laid out on the floor for anyone who felt like staying. I thought then that Father Callahan's love for my mother was mystical – almost abstract – like his love of the blood of the Martyrs – like his worship of the Saints. I felt that there was pain in his love and some deep reconciliation to loss. Whatever Father Callahan really felt for my mother, I was only glad at that time that it seemed to extend to me as my mother's daughter. He spoke only to me in the evenings. Father Callahan never seemed able to interest my mother. She would smile at him sometimes when she was sitting at her piano. But then when she was playing she quite often smiled at anyone who happened to be sitting around drinking in her drawing-room. She smiled, but it was as though she did not really see them. She certainly very rarely took the trouble to come over to address one word to him, and I often wondered why she kept on inviting him. She told me once that to dream about priests was very bad – that even if you dreamt about the Devil, it was much, much better. She also said that she hoped that I would never accept any gift from Father Callahan – even if it was something as small as a halfpenny or a handkerchief – for any gift from a priest could bring the most atrocious bad luck. 'And that's about all we need,' she said.

'What do you mean?' I asked her.

'When you are older,' she answered, staring out through the window to the waterfall, 'you will start to find out that very many things – can have very many meanings.'

'Shall I get you a cup of tea?' I asked her. I always disliked it when she started to speak in riddles. And she seemed so restless that day, unable even to settle down to her piano. I saw the disgust in her eyes and I knew that I had disappointed her. 'Yes,' she snapped at me, 'I suppose that you really might as well do just that!'

'You live too much in the past, Theresa,' my husband very often tells me. I wonder if I do. And I wonder if George notices where I really live, just so long as he can still see me sitting in my chair in his expensive West Side apartment. More and more I feel like that crusader that as a child I always hated so – that repulsive little Irish crusader who lay in his open coffin and had his hand shaken by tourists in the vaults of St Michan's in Dublin. 'It is one of the miracles what has preserved him here without embalmment!' the guide was always saying. And surely some guide seeing me sitting with George in our living-room could very well say the same about me now. My mother so loved those terrible musty vaults of St Michan's. She said that they still contained the lovely spirit of Parnell because he had once been laid out in state there. Sometimes she would take me down to visit them as often as three times a week. 'Shake the crusader's hand for luck, Theresa!' And I still remember the feel of his hand – so cold – so smooth – so shiny: the feel of a well-soaped saddle. 'As you see, the human nail continues growing after death,' the guide would keep on pattering. Those dreadful nails! The nails of a society woman – but so much yellower and almost as long as the chicken-bone fingers they were sprouting out of. Sometimes my mother said that she wished my father could have been buried under the church of St Michan's. 'He would have been with us still.' And I was always guiltily glad that she had never got her wish. I remember that the lights once fused when I was down in those tombs with my mother. We were forced to stand there in the darkness for nearly an hour while the guide, who was always stocious drunk, stumbled around cursing while he tried to find the fuse-box. My mother never stopped screaming. She said that she had felt the crusader brush her spine with his finger-nail. All the same the next week she was saying it was always beautiful to shake the hand of History. And very soon we were both back down there again.

'It seems to me that it really was your own lights that fused when you were down in those goddam tombs with your mother!' George sometimes says to me. 'It's sick, Theresa! It's really sick the way you live so much in the past!' But often while I potter round his apartment in the daytime, and often in the evenings while I sit watching him as he watches his favourite Late-Late Show while he files his toe-nails with his nail-file, I do not feel that I live in the past. Like that dismal little crusader I still have a hand which anyone can shake if they feel inclined to – but quite frequently I feel that I do not really live at all.

'You ought to see an analyst, Theresa. You reject everything. It's as if you feel that nothing can ever be so miraculous as all the old times that you spent with your screwy nut-case of a mother and her bunch of provincial Irish bull-shit artists. You are utterly out of touch with reality. You really seem to live in some kind of a crazy Celtic twilight . . .' I listen very attentively to all my husband's criticism. Now I may very well live in some kind of a twilight. But in a Celtic one? That I wonder . . . George often has a curious imprecision when it comes to using words. I watch George sitting with his head in his hands while he tries to think up some advertising slogan for sanitary-towels.

'Soft – Soft – Thistle-down Soft! Eliminates all fear of those tell-tale bulges!'
'It's beautiful George! It really has quite an amazing lyrical freshness!' 'I
don't need any of your boring patronage, Theresa. Look, you are a woman –
you ought to know about sanitary-towels. Don't just sit there acting so goddam
superior. For Christ's sake just try for once and give me a little bit of help!'
I look at him sitting there paralysed like some great podgy slow-witted school-
boy who has got hopelessly stuck in his lessons. 'Have you thought about Baby-
bottom Soft, George? Maybe that would be even better than Thistle-down.' He
considers it. And for one moment we are almost quite close. We suddenly have
a bond. We are suddenly a team. But then George shakes his head. 'One thing
I'll say for you, Theresa. You are certainly never the slightest fucking help.'

'Feeling sorry for yourself is your only full-time profession!' that poet of
the sanitary-towel sometimes shouts at me. 'How you love yourself, Theresa –
just yourself – and only really ever yourself!' 'How you love Our Lady!' my
mother said to me one night when I was sitting talking to Father Callahan in
her drawing-room. She rolled her huge beautiful eyes so scornfully down his
long black trailing skirts and then she laughed really maliciously. 'I wonder,'
she said, 'just how long you will be able to keep that up!' Father Callahan
never seemed to hear her when she spoke like that, although the blood crept out
from behind his ears and trickled down towards his nose like some slow
advancing army. And soon she was back at her piano and had forgotten him.
'O Boyne, once famed for battles, sport and conflicts, And great heroes of the
race of Conn,' she would moan, 'Art thou grey after all thy blooms? O aged
woman of grey-green pools, O wretched Boyne of many tears!' Father Callahan
would sit beside me and stare into her fire with his sad bloodshot eyes and
speak to me of life, and death, and the nature of humility and evil, and of the
Divine Perfections. Quite often he would say that all he prayed for me was
that when I was a little older I would still have the strength to remain 'white'.
'White? What is white?' I would ask him, although I knew well enough from
the girls of my convent, and I only wanted to hear him explain it. 'You will
know, my daughter. You will know in your time,' he always answered me,
pouring himself another brandy. Sometimes he would start to speak so intensely
that I really could not follow what he was saying, and frequently his soft voice
was completely wiped out by all the clash of glasses, and bottles and opinions,
and the thunderous wail of my mother's singing, but often, while he was speaking to me and I kept drinking her excellent red French wine, Father Callahan's
dark clerical clothes started to look brighter to me than all the brilliant silks
and velvets of my mother's friends, and I felt that it was of no importance that

73

he was a priest, and that I was a child, for we were like two disembodied spirits who had found such perfect harmony that it was impossible for anything ever to break it – and therefore nothing again could ever make me feel afraid.

Sometimes my mother would suddenly jump up from her piano and start screaming at all her guests. She would tell them that they were all just a gaggle of geese-like fools. She said she felt she would die unless she breathed some fresh air, and could hear the sound of water. And then she would grab Paddy Devlin or any other man who was still able to stand by the hand and drag him out through the door and take him down to the waterfall. Father Callahan always became very agitated when she behaved like this, although none of her other guests seemed to take much offence at her insults. Indeed a lot of them were usually sprawling half-asleep on the carpet at the time, or else locked away in some of the lavatories vomiting, and I doubt that they remembered all her abuse by morning. But Father Callahan always became very tense and miserable. He never seemed to be able to concentrate on conversation while my mother was out somewhere lost in the darkness. Often she would stay outdoors for what seemed like hours, and the whole time Father Callahan would never stop flicking his eyes towards the door, like a dog that keeps waiting for the return of its master. Once when my mother had stayed out even longer than usual, Father Callahan suddenly started quoting to me for no particular reason from his favourite Cardinal Newman. 'The Catholic Church holds it better for the sun and moon to drop from Heaven, for the earth to fail and for all the many millions on it to die of starvation in extremest agony, as far as temporal affliction goes, than that one soul, I will not say shall be lost, but should commit one single venial sin . . .' 'And where is the Charity in that, Father?' I asked him. 'There are very many enigmas,' he answered me irritably.

Were Father Callahan's enigmas all theological? Even now I feel that there are still so many questions. Even now I still keep asking myself – why did I never guess at that time – why did I never for one moment guess that there was something so elm-blighted, and most certainly enigmatical, behind all my mother's singing, and her quoting, and her over-hectic pagan laughter?

Father Callahan and Doctor Donovan were standing side by side in her drawing-room when I got back one day from my convent. The doctor was a very tall man, and seeing the priest standing beside him in his long dark trailing skirts, I remember thinking that Doctor Donovan looked rather like a bridegroom, and Father Callahan like his small black bride. Their faces looked strange – rigid – almost angry – and the sight of them made me feel afraid.

'Daughter, have courage.'

'What has happened?'

'Daughter, pray for strength. Remember it is only an ante-chamber.'

'What is only an ante-chamber, Father?' My heart was pounding. I thought for a moment that he was speaking of my mother's drawing-room.

'Life,' Father Callahan said slowly. 'Life, as you know, is only really just an ante-chamber to Eternity.'

'Has something happened to my mother?' I turned to the doctor. He was so silent. I saw his eyes flick nervously to Father Callahan. Why should he not answer me? He was such an old man. He was such a tall man. He was a doctor. Why could he not answer me without waiting for the priest?

'It's all over with her,' Father Callahan said. He looked different to me in the daylight. His face looked suddenly weak and blotchy – rather ordinary and unintelligent, like the faces of so many of the ill-nourished adolescents that always hung around the bar-tents at all the races. 'Let us kneel.' Father Callahan dropped down on his knees on my mother's drink-stained carpet and the doctor copied him a little awkwardly with his long stiff thighs. I remained standing. I remember staring at the curtains of the drawing-room. I had never noticed before that their scarlet velvet was so shabby. They were drooping down from their poles like limp, faded washing.

'Were you there, Father Callahan?' I asked him.

'I was.'

'Did she see you come.'

'She did indeed. The Lord was very merciful. She was conscious for nearly one hour.'

'But that is really terrible! She must have known why you had come!'

'She knew, of course.'

'But how could you have done that to her, Father Callahan? She must have hated to know. She must have been so absolutely terrified to know!'

'She wanted to know. But in any case she would have had to know. How could she be allowed to go in her sins?'

'But I don't understand how your mind worked, Father Callahan. I know that you never liked to face it – but you know just as well as I that she was never a believer. She despised priests. She despised what she called their doggerel. What use did you think you could be to someone like that? She must have felt a total panic at the very sight of you arriving so horribly final and chilling in your black. Maybe she still had a little hope until she saw you. I wish that you had never let me know the terrible thing that you did to her. Oh, why couldn't you have just kept away from her?'

'I tell you my child that when she saw me, she was glad. My presence in her agony was a consolation. It is to them all.'

'But maybe she wouldn't have needed any consolation, Father Callahan, not if you had never made her know only too well why you had come.'

'You are speaking quite wildly, my child. It is your grief. You still know absolutely nothing of the facts.'

'But I know how much she hated to know anything unpleasant, Father Callahan. She was someone who cried if other people trod on wild flowers. She was never in the least bit brave. Is that not true, Doctor Donovan? You remember that she was even terrified of injections. She could never bear to know when they were coming. She always stuck her arm out as far as it would go – and she turned her head away – and squeezed her eyes tight shut. The way she would scream and moan – it was really quite horrible to hear it – and always long before the needle had even gone into her!'

'My child, you seem quite demented. You are speaking of things which are quite beside the point.'

'You knew her, Father Callahan!' I started crying. 'You came to our house every evening. You knew what she was like. You loved her. You know very well that she would have wanted to go like an animal – like a butterfly – knowing nothing. Even if she had no chance – why couldn't you have allowed her to go on still believing that she had some tiny chance? I know that her hopes must have been hopeless. But what right did you have to take those last little hopes away from her? I will never understand how you had the cruelty to do that to her!'

'Don't speak disrespectfully to the Father!' Doctor Donovan suddenly snapped at me from his kneeling position on the carpet.

'She is not railing at me. She is only railing at me as the vessel of something so much higher that it passes her comprehension.' Father Callahan looked exhausted and the blotches on his face were becoming so brilliant that they resembled a disease.

'I tell you, my child, that she was serene. When it finally came to her, there was very little struggle. The end is often not at all like you imagine. It is often somewhat of an anti-climax.'

'An anti-climax!' I saw him shiver as I screamed at him. 'For you it may have well seemed like an anti-climax, Father Callahan. But I hardly think that it could have seemed very much like that to her. She was not a priest you know, Father Callahan. She loved all sorts of things. She loved love – she loved water – she loved poetry – she loved music. She was someone who loved life!'

'She can't have loved life as much as you imagine.' Father Callahan bent his head in prayer. 'May the Lord have mercy on her.'

'What makes you say that?'

'It was horrible . . . But she couldn't be blamed. Something must have entered into her. She wasn't herself. She just turned on herself. She died of her wounds. She grabbed a carving-knife. Her real self can't have been with her. It was plain at the end that she never intended it. She was the one that sent for Doctor Donovan. He did all that could be done for her. But she had been too savage . . .'

Fact

WOMEN'S THEATRE*

As though a Women's Institute fête had been expecting a visit from the Queen and had only been informed after it opened that she was confined to her bed with a heavy cold, a feeling of let-down hung over the Women's Lib rally. Where would the spark come from now? All the goods laid out on the stalls looked suddenly second-hand and shoddy; the band was still playing but now it seemed amateurish and out of tune.

'Where's Kate Millett?'

'Which one's Millett?'

'That can't be her. That's a man, you fool!'

It was smoky, claustrophobic and hot, sitting on the hard benches in the Open Space Theatre.

'What does Millett look like anyway?'

'A sort of dumpy Mary McCarthy. But they say she's not coming . . . They say that on Friday she saw the play.'

We too had just seen the play. 'Holocaust Theatre is the real end of a nightmare,' Jane Arden, its author, had claimed in a programme note. But did the audience agree with her, who had sat in a circle for what seemed like so many hours? Surely Jane Arden, with the rhapsodic rhetoric to which we had all now become accustomed, would be the first to say that endness was only really fractured beginningness and all part of the nuclear feminine-masculine principles which it would take a thousand years to sort out.

The meeting was starting in earnest. In the same centre of the same stage where there had just been eight extremist women writhing naked while they moaned and masturbated, and complained that they were oxen and had 'holes inside', there were now four more women – but they were moderates. Edna O'Brien, Anne Sharpley of the *Daily Mail*, Jill Tweedie of the *Guardian*, and their chairwoman Mrs George Orwell. Unlike the previous female cast they were all sitting on chairs instead of potties. If they had holes inside, one sensed

*Written in 1971.

F

oh? so what's knew.

immediately that they would be the very last to mention them. They had serious-looking pencils and papers and a table. They spoke the language of the *Observer* and the *New Statesman* rather than the Underground. Clearly, if they were to have their way, there would be no more talk of 'milky breasts and the music that sings from these contained vessels'. They wanted orderly and constructive discussion of the need for nursery schools and equal opportunity and pay for women. They wanted the meeting conducted as it might have been if Kate Millett had been present — if only she had not seen the play!

But their chairwoman Mrs George Orwell was a Kerensky and was to prove totally unable to control the harsh forces of chaos and revolution which were to unseat her from below. She opened the discussion by suggesting that the audience were gathered there tonight to discuss the various socio-economic problems confronting women in 1971. Instantly a hippy, a man hippy, with a Vanessa Redgrave white-bandaged head and a white bunny rabbit embroidered on his arm, appeared very much like a conjuror's bunny and seated himself at the conference table. It was assumed by some of the audience that he was a proper member of the Women's Liberation panel, that he had been invited to join them in the interests of democratic liberality. But this was not the case. He was doing some kind of an aggressive sit-in, something perilously near to a grope-in. He was only there because he wanted to be allowed to do his thing. Mrs Orwell, gallant and foolhardy, tried to ignore him just as she seemed to feel she could afford to ignore the restless, menacing mood which was already stirring in the little basement theatre stuffed thick with women. She went on talking pleasantly. The women watched her, and waited. Their faces were implacable and their eyes had the ruthless glitter of the *tricoteuses*.

There they all sat, the solid phalanxes of card-carrying members of Women's Liberation and the more virile rows of ladies from Gay Liberation. There were many old-timers — pioneers of the Movement with cropped hoary heads and far more muscle than any stevedore. They had the very same physique as the ancient bull-dykes who were once employed as throwers-out in the tourist lesbian night-clubs of Berlin and Paris in the Twenties. What interest could they possibly have in Mrs Orwell's cheery talk of nursery schools? They had fought alone on their barricades throughout the old dark days of the sexual Depression. Surely, to them, Holocaust Theatre must seem like apricot purée for babies. What man would have ever cared or dared to challenge one of them alone on a dark night? What man would dare to challenge their daughters, the new little Gay Lib girls? They were as hard and springy as wire-wool with their hair quiffed up like messenger boys and heavily oiled with men's hair-lotion.

They seemed to be all boots and studded leather, sitting there with their thuggish little deliberately delinquent faces in deliberately defiant couples.

On the back benches behind the two main parties were ranged the great blocks of unaffiliated sympathisers who were wearing anything from kaftans to hot pants. Many looked a little bovine, neither over-zealous nor over-intelligent. Lumpen Lib. The cast of Holocaust Theatre were mingled with them and still wore the straitjackets and lunatic-asylum apparel — symbols for male oppression — that they had worn for the play. There also seemed to be a lot of women from America, and here and there, like rare chaff, a sprinkling of men.

Mrs Orwell smiled engagingly at her motley audience and told them that she didn't believe in all this stuff about female oppression — that she had never known a case of a couple who were in love where one of them had ever tried to dominate the other. From the back a man muttered that he had never known a case where one of them didn't. But he kept his voice down, there in the catacombs of Women's Lib.

'The real thing now,' Mrs Orwell went on firmly, 'is how are we meant to bring up our children? Must little boys still be brought up as manly little boys, and little girls like pretty little girls?' Was Mrs Orwell deliberately tempting her fate? She was acting as chairwoman to an occasion which was surely intended to promote the opening of the world's first real 'Women's Theatre'. And yet, as though it was an unmentionable bad smell, she had still not made a single reference to the play.

A member of her panel agreed with Mrs Orwell and said that the point of a meeting like this should be a heightened consciousness of what it meant to be female. And this remark seemed to do it. Suddenly from the back benches there was a horrible, haunting howl, as though one of the women there had gone into labour. It was the authoress. It was Jane Arden, who had written *A New Communion for Freaks, Prophets and Witches* and had invented Holocaust Theatre.

She was standing up with her blazing eyes and her tousled gypsy's hair and she was waving the fist of the rising worker. 'Your panel is all shit! What are all you women doing sitting there at that table? What is this — a bloody boardroom? Get off your chairs and come and meet us! We are all oppressed! We want the whole bloody society torn up by its roots! We are on the edge of a new dimension! Don't you see the holocaust is here? I have a black man sitting here next to me. And he is oppressed.' A little shiver of unease went through the liberal wing of Lib. Did he like being called a black man by Jane Arden? The whole meeting turned and stared at him. She had made him look so nervous. But for all anyone knew, he might well be a 'fascist male' black man.

'Shit! Shit!' she chanted. The clock seemed to have been turned back an hour and we were listening again to the monotonous complaining choruses of her play: 'Desolation! Scrubbing! Oxen! Fracture! Shit!' 'Everything you have all been saying is just bloody bourgeois shit!' she screamed at the panel. No one really seemed to have said very much so far. No one was ever going to be allowed to say anything very much for the rest of the meeting. Mrs Orwell agreed that Jane Arden was right when she said that this was holocaust. 'Hear! Hear!' called the audience each time Jane Arden yelled 'Shit!'

'Now that's quite enough, thank you,' Mrs Orwell said and she tapped grimly for order on her table. Edna O'Brien was just able to murmur that she thought that there were no men, and no women, and no children, that there was just 'to be'. And then the hippy jumped up with his bandaged head, looking like Victorian pictures of the risen Christ, and embarked on a filibuster. 'The whole structure of society is rotten. The whole structure stinks. The whole structure is sterile and rotten and it stinks.' On and on his hippy bromides rolled. Was there someone who could stop him? Edna O'Brien tried by leaning over and patting him on the back as if he was a begging dog who was clawing her leg. Mrs Orwell tried to interrupt him and make one last shot to get back to baby-sitting and equal pay. He turned on her with the snarl of a dog. 'You shut up!' he said. 'Oh man, you better just shut up!'

The cannon rumble of 'Shit! Shit!' was starting again. Then two granite-tough butch figures from Gay Lib leapt up from their seats and linked arms, and, purposeful as two traffic-wardens who have spotted a badly parked car, they started walking towards the hippy. He might soon wish he had never spoken a word at a Women's Lib meeting, never made a single mention of the fabric of society. He now looked as vulnerable as the fragile rotten structure he had talked so much about. They came up to him and spat in his face and hissed: 'You prick! Oh you bloody prick!' He went scurrying away and sat cross-legged on the floor and for the rest of the evening seemed to be sulking and meditating.

Later Jane Arden was to complain that Mrs Orwell and her panel of 'liberal democrats' wrecked the 'ripple'. But after the rout of the hippy they seemed to lose all power to control it. From every part of the hall women were jumping up and starting to scream all at once. No speaker seemed to agree on any single point with any other speaker. No speaker ever allowed any other speaker to finish. A woman seemed to be saying that every time she washed her hus-

84

band's underpants she kept thinking that no one had ever washed hers. Another was shouting that she was here tonight because she was a victim of male domination. From the stuffy standing ranks at the back of the hall more and more women were trying uselessly to get a hearing. The French Women's Liberationists are asking that a wreath be placed under the Arc de Triomphe in honour of the wife of the unknown soldier. Was someone now trying to ask for an English equivalent? Were members of Gay Lib trying to make their usual demand that lesbians get the legal right to sue for alienation of affection? How could you tell when someone was yelling so much louder that they wanted the destruction of the nuclear family, someone else that they wanted a redefinition of the female role?

A pretty working-class mother tried to say that she had three kids hanging onto her skirts and her problem was how she could ever get out of the house. Jane Arden had said all the women at this meeting were on the edge of a new dimension and in this moment of liberated lunacy who could dare to bring up something quite as boring as their baby-sitting problems? A man got up and asked if he could read a statement. 'It is not always an unadulterated joy to be in possession of a cock.' He was loudly hissed and booed. Someone was screaming that men should be forbidden to speak. 'Make them learn what it's like to have to listen to women!' A man said he had had a mother and two wives and he couldn't remember doing anything else all his life. He then walked out. The 'black man' tried to express sympathy and solidarity with the women. He said he had found that the breasts of one of the actresses who had stripped naked in the play were exactly the right size. Was he aware of the full enormity of his *faux pas*? Had he simply misunderstood the whole point of the play? Had he not grasped that when that actress exposed her breasts it was meant to be the tragic high point of the whole evening — that her poor naked nipples had symbolised woman's degradation, misery and exploitation throughout the millennia? He seemed hurt and puzzled by the storm of booing. Did he feel so aggrieved because he knew he was the only person who had made any attempt to say that they liked the play?

From the start only a hissing and rather hysterical hatred of men had ever really unified this disgruntled audience. Quite suddenly this hatred directed itself full force onto Mrs Orwell and her bland panel: 'You with your bloody bourgeois jobs and your husbands and all your au pairs!' Two avenging furies from Women's Gay Lib marched towards them goose-stepping like Prussian soldiers. Their great boots struck sparks from the floor. They picked up the panel's heavy trestle table as though it was a piece of tissue paper and lifted it high in the air as if they were performing some complicated modern ballet. Were they going to smash it down on the heads of the flustered panel? There was certainly a feeling now that only a little ritual blood-letting could provide them in their frustrations with any real catharsis. But they only carried it rather tamely to the other side of the stage. 'You bloody pricks!' Their disgust with the panel extended to the entire audience. Even their great army boots seemed quite revolted as they clumped out down the aisle.

There is almost nothing that looks quite so embarrassingly naked as a debating panel which has been suddenly stripped of its table. Even the actresses of Holocaust Theatre in the most poignant moments of the play, when they bared their breasts to show their female abasement, never looked nearly as nude and degraded as Mrs Orwell and her committee. Their very nylonned knees, spotlit, seemed indecently exposed. They sat stunned, and as though trapped in invisible stocks.

A woman came running down the aisle waving her arms for silence. She was the manageress of the Open Space Theatre. She seemed to be very deeply distressed. She said that she had made considerable sacrifices to put on this Woman's play, to allow her theatre to be used for this discussion, and the disgraceful behaviour of the women who had attended had made her deeply regret what she had done.

Now that the panel, the symbol of order, was deposed, some of the women went on shouting 'shit' and 'prick' and expressing various unintelligible grievances, but the fun had gone out of it. The rally broke up and there was only the horrible flatness and frustration that often falls after the Demo, when even the most militant start to realise that the pigs are still in power and really very little has changed.

The next day I talked to Jane Arden at her house in London. Before she invented the Holocaust Theatre, her most famous play was *Vagina Rex*. She sat facing me on the floor wearing a kaftan. She looked rather beautiful, and she spoke with intensity, at great speed, using the druggy rhetoric of the Underground. The word she seemed to use most frequently was 'impacted' – a word I had previously associated only with wisdom teeth. She kept applying it to society, to emotions, to the female role and the nuclear family, and I kept on visualising all these things, with far too many roots sunk deep in someone's gum.

She too had found the rally disgraceful: it had just been a 'bank of fragmented language'. I would have expected that in some way she would have found such a 'bank' to be rather nicely 'unimpacted'. But it appeared that she had felt outraged that her Holocaust Theatre had not been made 'central to the discussion'. She was bitter about Mrs Orwell and the way in which she had chaired the meeting: 'that woman' and her bunch of 'liberal democrats' had ruined all the 'vibes'.

I asked her what she would have done if she had chaired such a meeting. Her head tossed — she found the question stupid: 'I would have allowed the vibrations to enact. I would have tried to seal off the abscesses. I would have had a show of hands. A show of hands always means vibrations. It always means: "It's me." "It's me" is what revolution in the real sense is really about. I would have asked: "How many of you here are fragmented? How many of you here fear death? How many of you here feel impacted? How many of you wake up and want to scream in the night?" Women are changed once they see Holocaust Theatre. Once you have cracked their boxed-in, fractured processes of thinking they can never be the same again. I hate Germaine Greer because she retreats from her humiliation. The real poets of oppression have to be grafted onto their oppression. I am much more identified with exploitation.'

She saw me looking round her large and luxurious house, which stands on the Little Venice Canal, only a few doors from Lady Diana Cooper's. 'I know I don't look very exploited outside, but I still feel it inside. I'm not separate from my work of art. Every nerve centre in Holocaust is me.' She said that American women and members of Gay Lib seemed especially 'open' to Holocaust, and that Kate Millett herself had been very 'responsive' and had deplored the lack of a similar theatre in the USA. She became messianic: 'I woke up one morning and suddenly I knew that I had to stop masturbating in my fantasies — that I'd go mad if I didn't reach out to women. All my judgments have always been formed by my vibrations and I knew it was the moment to start the ripple. I got onto the telephone and gathered a great group of women together. I asked them if they were prepared to be totally committed to me and my idea. I warned them that if they followed me, everything else they cared for in their lives would have to go.'

'How many stepped forward?'

'Only the eight who are now playing at the Open Space. Women are so horribly timorous. It's their conditioning.'

'Did any of the women who stepped forward have children?'

'Some of them had kids, certainly.' She went on. 'The Church has failed women — I can give them a way to work out their rituals. I've always been someone who would stand on her head to make things richer.'

PORTRAIT OF THE BEATNIK*

Almost every day in some newspaper or magazine, the American Housewife makes her new complaint. A Beatnik philosopher has told her that she lives in 'the Age of the White Rhinoceros,' and another has told her that it is 'the Age of Fried Shoes.' 'Where,' she asked, 'is all this Beatnik Movement leading us?' Her question is gratuitous. There has never been a Movement, merely a mirage, merely a masquerade.

The Beatnik is simply a bourgeois fantasy that has become incarnated and incarcerated, in a coffee-house and a 'pad'; he is merely the Bohemian in every American business-man that has got out. He is a luxury product, the revolutionary who offers no threat, the nonconformist whose nonconformity is commercial. He shocks and scandalises without creating anxiety; he is the rebel not without cause, but the rebel without repercussion.

Supposedly revolutionary, the 'Beatnik Movement' is unique in that it enjoys the recognition, the support, and succour of the very society whose dictates it pretends to flout. It has all the trappings of the subversive, the meeting in the darkened cellar, the conspiratorial whisper behind the candle in the chianti bottle, the nihilistic mutter, without the mildest element of subversion. No one in the future, when filling in an official form, will ever be made to swear that they have never been a Beatnik.

The American working man is unconcerned with the Beat Generation and its quest for 'the primitive Beginnings.' The Beatnik scandalises and interests only the middle-class public from which he springs. As opposed to the Bum (who might well be said to be more truly Beat) he is quite popular. He presents no obvious social incitement or question. He is 'cool' and polite. Whereas the Bum rolls in the streets of downtown Los Angeles, drunk and cursing, the Beatnik sits peacefully in his coffee-house, nonconforming over capuccino, a safely-licensed anarchist. Everyone knows where to find him: he is always in his Beatnik Joint or in his 'pad'. Everyone knows who he is because of his beard, and *Life* Magazine can photograph him whenever it wishes.

Unlike the delinquent (with whom he is often confused), the Beatnik only ever troubles the Police over the technical issue of whether or not, if he reads

*Written in 1964.

88 ✝ haven't heard that word for Years

his own poem to Jazz in a coffee-house, it constitutes 'entertainment' and there-fore invokes the need for an entertainment licence.

The Beatnik in his bold rebellion against American Bourgois Values, is about as dangerous as the three revolutionaries in Orwell's *1984*. Like them, he has been put by the State safely in front of a chess-set in the Chestnut Tree Café, and there he is allowed to sit being revolutionary.

The Beat Generation has declared that it will take no part in the 'middle-class rat race'; it has protested 'a sacred dedication to poverty'; it has denounced all Western civilisation as 'square shuck' (phoney).

A popular misconception is that the term 'Beatnik' signifies one who is *beat* in the sense of 'down beat', or 'licked' – whereas to the Beat Generation it signifies 'the beatific one.'

The ego-ideal of the Beatnik is the 'cool hipster' – the man who sits detached with his own flask in his own hip pocket, the man who is 'way out', the man who doesn't 'wig' (care), the man who finds beatitude in noncommit-ment.

The 'square' is often not 'hip' to the fact that despite similarities of dress, the Beatnik is by no means his existentialist predecessor. An obscure Beat philosopher finally clarified this point when he said, 'The existentialist cat dug like that the positive answer of nothingness, in the face of nothingness, is positivism – we dig that the positive answer of nothingness, to nothingness, is nothingness – Man, isn't that farther out?'

The Beatnik rejects articulateness, speech involving a conversational com-mitment constituting lack of 'coolness.' Paradoxically, therefore, the Beat Generation can only speak in order to say that it will not speak, and Jack Kerouac and Alan Ginsberg who are generally known as the Beat spokesmen, are by very definition, as well as by their success and achievements, nonhipsters.

Ideally, a truly 'cool cat' should be *completely* self-contained and therefore *completely* silent. The average Beatnik compromises, however, by speaking in language cut to the maximum. His talk, an abbreviated version of already abbreviated Jazz talk, amounts to complete code. A 'T.O.,' for example, is a much-used Beat word for a rich society woman who questions prostitutes, with half-thrilled envy, about the physical mechanics of their trade. An amateur hipster might be trapped into thinking that a 'T.O.' was an initiate, for it derives from 'To be turned out,' meaning initiated, deriving from 'To be turned on,' referring to 'On pot,' which stems in turn from 'on the pod' of marijuana. The expression is now, however, *only* used to describe not the initiate but the would-be but too-afraid initiate. It is often claimed by the

Beatniks that many women living in Park Avenue pent-houses, and many wives of successful movie stars living in Beverly Hills mansions, are secret 'T.O.'s' in regard to Beat.

No professor of semantics could be more severe about misuse of vernacular than the hipster. The charlatan can be spotted instantly, and denounced as a 'square'. He often, for example, makes incorrect use of the term 'to ball' which (in the 'forties) meant to make love. Now, however, the expression 'I balled the cat' could only mean to the truly Beat, that you were grateful to someone, so grateful in fact that you would only have *liked* to have balled them in the old-fashioned sense.

Beatific talk is the very soul of brevity, if not wit. It is deliberately functional, for the hipster rejects euphemism. He 'sets a scene' when he tells, 'wigs' when he's worried, 'gigs' when he works, 'bugs' when he's annoyed, 'wails' when he functions, 'floats' when he's drunk, 'grazes' when he's content, 'bends' when he's tired, 'scenes' when he arrives, 'splits' when he goes.

The Beatnik, in his rejection of the popular American concept that Success equates with Manhood, stresses a non-virility often mistaken for homosexuality. He is essentially a-sexual. Once again the ideal of the 'cool' precluding the personal commitment demanded by sexual activity. He has, however, no particular objection to sexual intercourse as long as it is conducted quickly, clinically, and above all wordlessly. The Beat 'cat' approaches the Beat 'chick' with the ritualistic 'Pad me' – his 'Pad' being his home where he keeps his foam rubber mattress. The 'chick' can either reply 'Dig' (a sign of cool acquiescence), or otherwise she can merely snap 'Drop!' (a much-used abbreviation of 'Drop dead'). In reverse, the 'chick's' approach to the male is equally formalised; she must say 'I'm frigid,' to which he can either reply 'I'll make you wail' (function) or, otherwise, 'Don't bug.'

Despite his rejection of marriage as middle-class 'shuck' (phoney), the Beatnik's Wedding is an important event in any Beat community. He marries in the Ocean, only at midnight. He and his Beat Bride-to-be stand naked in the waves while the rites are performed by a Beatific friend who reads a self-composed hymeneal ritual poem, which is then followed by a lunar incantation. The Bridegroom then silently hands the 'chick' a ring of flowers which she must throw into the waves in order to symbolise that her hipster is giving himself to 'The real mama, the Ocean, the mama of the whole race of Man,' while she is herself uniting with 'The Old Man of the Sea'.

Non-Beatnik grandmothers and aunts are invited to attend these services, and often leave in tears before the wedding breakfast, which naturally takes place in a 'pad' and is as formal as the Sea Wedding. The newly-weds sit in a semi-circle composed of silently contemplative friends, 'light up on muggles' (smoke marijuana), and continue their search for 'the inner luminous experience.'

Beat philosophy is misty, mystical, and eclectic. Claiming to embrace Zen, the Beatnik philosopher paradoxically rejects discipline; he therefore replaces the Zen Ideal of a total commitment to the moment by a Beat ideal of a striving towards a state of totally noncommited contemplation. As a result he often merely arrives at a condition very similar to the one in which the American Housewife watches her television.

He prefers Jung to Freud, the concept of the collective, as opposed to the personal, subconscious being *'cooler'* in the sense that it predisposes less commitment to self. Other influences on his thought have been St Francis of Assisi, Nietzsche, Ouspenski, and St John of the Cross. He admires Joyce for his obscurity.

Within the confines that he has set himself, the Beatnik adheres to his conventions of nonconventionality with the enthusiasm of the Rotarian Club member for his rules. Every hipster wears the strict uniform of classical Bohemianism. He is heavily bearded. He has an open sandal, a chunky raw-wool sweater, and a little leather cap with a button on it. All his clothes *must* be bought second-hand. A similar Beat regulation is that his 'pad' or mattress must be acquired *only* from the Salvation Army. Beds are considered 'square' so it must therefore be put straight on the floor of his 'pad' which is also his home, and ideally should be a battered shack. He must also hand-paint his floorboards with enigmatic and abstract (*'way-out'*) designs, for one of his slogans is *'In the meaningless lies the meaning.'*

The true Beatnik should never 'hustle' (do any paid work). He must sleep all day and only emerge by night. In the corner of every Beat 'pad' there must necessarily be a gigantic stack of unwashed dishes.

As a deliberate reaction against the Hollywood emphasis on the breast and the flashing lipsticked smile, the appearance of his female Beatnik is characterised by a studied and aggressive a-sexuality. Pale-lipped and unsmiling she sits in a high-necked shapeless tunic made of woven wool. Her legs must always be crossed and heavily encased in black woolly stockings. Her cheeks are whitened with thick, white make-up base, her hair hangs dank and darkly jagged. She is to be seen nightly alone, staring over an unplayed chess-game with a mystic and heavily mascara'd eye.

In order to ensure the correct attire of visitors, many a Beatnik coffee-house has an adjoining dress shop : a Beatnik boutique. There, on sale, are elaborately-designed thirty-dollar Beat Generation tunics made of raw Mexican wool, sackcloth shirts, primitive leather water-pouches, and Beat jewellery made of iron.

I spoke with an ex-Beatnik turned Beat dress designer. She sat in her workshop and sewed the thong on a raw-hide sandal. She spoke of her Beat past with the apologetic nostalgia sometimes found in retired members of the Communist Party. 'Jesus, I dug Beatific – Man, the swinginest [it's the best] – I like dug splittin' [I felt obliged to leave it] – I dug giggin' for bread to wail [I was obliged to work for the money to go on functioning]. . . .'

Her friend, another renegade Beatnik, who was sitting in the corner painting papier-mâché model figurines of Beatniks (later to be sold in a boutique) was less enthusiastic about the Movement. 'Beatific's a bug,' she said.

The Beat coffee-houses are characterised by their extreme gloom, and by their cathedral silences. They attract not only the hipster but also the wandering psychotic who gets mistaken for Beat because he is 'way out'. They also shelter two unfortunate by-products of Beat. First, the Bogus Beatnik : the Hollywood agent and the successful car-salesman, who, having worked by day go corruptly Beat by night. Secondly, the hypocritical hipster, who, unaware of the deeper philosophical significance of the Movement, has taken out 'Beat' as he might take out an insurance policy, merely to protect himself against any future censor from a success-worshipping society. Failure is impossible to anyone who is Beat, for they have rejected aspiration.

The entertainment at the Beat coffee-house consists of 'Prose and Poetry readings' and folk-singing, the latter being part of the quest for the 'primitive beginnings'. No alcohol is served, for the Beatnik rejects 'lushing' (drinking) as part of bourgeois 'shuck'.

Short, silent, home-made Beat movies are also shown. As there would appear to be only a limited number of these films, the more popular and 'farther out' ones are shown up to four or five times on the same night. An old man looms upon the screen, huge and fearful. The camera remains lengthily upon the vast cigar which he holds between his teeth. An adolescent appears, white-faced and knuckle-clenching, his eyes roll, his face contorts. The Jazz background music mounts to a crescendo. The boy splits a gut (laughs), he lifts his hand, and with a sudden frenzied violence, strikes the cigar from the old man's mouth. The camera follows the cigar which rolls in the dust. The old man shivers. He rocks, holding his head in agony. He staggers to a lavatory. He vomits. The camera remains upon the lavatory pan until it slowly dissolves into a vagina. The audience slowly turn their heads to see if everyone else is 'hip.' A voice always says, 'Dig that crazy sequence!'

Between the runnings of films, Beatific poem-reading takes place to the accompaniment of Bongo drums.

> *The take-off*
> > *on one*
> > > *and*
>
> *a half*
> > *push up*
>
> *not all*
> > *at once*
> > *just cool*
>
> *hip.*

The unsuspecting tourist suffering from the 'square' illusion that it is possible to drop in at a coffee-house for only a few minutes, then becomes 'hip' to his error. Once 'Beat readings' are in progress only someone with the courage or the insensitivity that would enable him to leave the front pew of an Anglican church while the parson is delivering his Easter sermon, can even conceive of making an exit under the condemnatory scrutiny of the Beatific congregation's culturally pious eye.

The tourist often finds towards dawn (for there is an important Beat tenet: *'Night sleep is for Squares'*) that after a whole evening on capuccino and 'Modigliani's' (described on Beat menus as 'Murals of ham and gherkin on rye'), he is slowly becoming 'cooler and cooler', and 'further and further out'.

The 'entertainment' often ends with a famous Beat musician, Lord Buckley, giving a nasal rendering of the story of Jesus of Nazareth walking on the waters. *And der Naz said, 'Walk cool, Baby, walk cool. . . .'*

Ever since the publication of *On the Road,* which focused upon the Beatnik a furore of public interest and attention, Jack Kerouac's right to the title of 'Father of the Beat Generation' has been jealously contested. Kenneth Rexroth, an elderly and obscure San Franciscan poet, made the first violent attempt to secure the title for himself when he protested angrily to the Press that he had been living all his life 'the kind of life that Kerouac just writes about'.

Another far more powerful figure then emerged in the form of a lesser-known (and therefore 'cooler') poet named Lawrence Lipton. A man approaching sixty, he denounced Kerouac for being in his 'thirties, and therefore unfitted to represent the Beat Generation who were essentially a product of the 1950's. He was appointed 'Grand Lama' in Venice West, a slum area of Los Angeles, where there are many suitably Beat and dilapidated shacks, and he is now hoping to establish it as the new Beat World Capital.

I spoke with the 'Grand Lama', he reclined on his 'pad' Pasha-like and smoked a cigar. 'Our pad,' he said, 'has the same symbolical importance to us, as did the couch of the Bohemians of the 'thirties. Beat, you will understand, my dear young woman, is far more than a religion. Beat, my dear young lady, is a way of Life.'

He closed his eyes.

'Here, down in Venice West,' he continued, 'we have a new kind of Beat, the real Beat, the Beat Generation of the future. I have called them by their true title, *The Holy Barbarians,* and the report that I have just finished making about them will be called by that very name. I have already received extensive enquiries about it, not only from the Book-of-the-Month Club, but also from several television programmes, the M.-G.-M. Studios, and many anthropologists from U.C.L.A. I tell you all this, you will understand, merely so that you will really grasp how big this whole thing is. Already my poems are being scribbled on the lavatory walls of New York, already our Movement is spreading to Japan, Italy, France, Germany, and Great Britain. The Holy Barbarians, you will see, my dear young woman, will very soon be of world-wide interest!'

We had a long silence.

'I,' he continued, speaking with a slow and portentous solemnity, 'am the Mentor of the Holy Barbarians. They call me *The Shaman of the Tribe.* I interpret their way of life to the public. I have probably made more tape-recordings of Beatnik conversations than any other living man.' He languidly waved his hand at a mountainous stack of tape spools lying on his floor. 'There,' he said, 'you have one hundred hours' worth of authentic Beat conversations, private philosophic conversations, you understand, taking place in simple pads, amongst young and simple people, but ones who are asking, more profoundly, more honestly than any previous generation, who they are, and where they are going. . . .'

Once again he closed his eyes. 'We, the Holy Barbarians, finding nothing in the West, have turned towards the East. We reject your Audens and your Spenders and all their affiliations. Our poets' Search goes inwards for The Luminous Experience. We reject and scorn your Angry Young Men with their social preoccupations. We seek much further for the non-political Answer.' 'The Lama' suddenly looked at me with a suspicious, visionary eye. 'That does not in the least mean to say,' he added quickly, 'that we do not utterly reject the Russian way of life. We in fact even have an expression amongst our hipsters, *There's no Square like a red Square.'*

Once again we had a silence. 'We, the Holy Barbarians, have totally rejected racial barriers,' he went on. 'We call a negro a *nigger* and a *spade,* for he knows we say the words with Love. You might really describe us in fact as a Community of individuals seeking only for The Beatific Vision, The Experience of Holiness, The Orgiastic Fulfilment, in Self. Our hipsters would say that we seek only *to flip our wings.*

'I'm afraid,' he said, suddenly smiling with scornful patronage, 'that that will have very little meaning to you.

'We,' he continued, making heavy use of the Papal *we,* 'might well be compared to the Early Christians. We are the Outlaws from the Social Lie. We are the Persecuted People, the Apocalyptic People, the Nocturnal People. The people of the night,' he added, for fear I had not understood.

As I was leaving, 'The Lama' stood in the doorway of his shack. 'We have many, many Artists down here in Venice West,' he said, 'all of them living in dedicated poverty. Some of them are among the most creative talents in America. I should very much like you to have a look at them. I will telephone you as soon as I have arranged to have you shown round their pads.' Suddenly I became cool, visionary. I saw that 'The Lama' had already, mystically, ruthlessly, appointed my future Duties. He had ordained how my life from then on was to be spent. Like a Florence Nightingale, or a conscientious Inspector of an Insane Asylum, making daily rounds of condemned Artists in padded cells.

HARLEM FREE SCHOOL

I was sitting in the class-room of a Mini Open Free School on the fringe of Harlem and I found that just one silly sentence, a child's tongue-twister, was suddenly repeating uselessly in my brain. 'Imagine an imaginary menagery manager managing an imaginary menagery.' *

They had told me that if I wanted to sit in on the class it was of the utmost importance that I arrive sharp at 10.15. They had made such a great point that they could only allow one journalist to attend the class for the presence of more than one onlooker might be disturbing. It had all sounded very reasonable. It had all sounded even a little formidable in its structured seriousness. But having arrived on the very dot of 10.15, I found that new and crazier versions of that stale old tongue-twister were already starting to go twisting through my mind. 'Imagine an imaginary onlooker disturbing an imaginary class.'

Already something seemed to be very wrong. 'Imagine an imaginary class disturbing an imaginary onlooker.' For already I felt very disturbed. I was there sitting in on the class, and the thing I found so deeply disturbing was that I could see absolutely no sign of any class. ○

There was something which very much resembled a menagery. Most certainly that was not imaginary. There was a room in which about fifty teenage blacks were roaming around screaming, and necking, and cursing, a room which had a floor which was carpeted with food-droppings, a room which was so incredibly littered and filthy that one felt if one were to touch anything in it one risked acquiring some unpleasant skin disease. There was a feeling of caged violence in the way that all these coloured teenagers were aimlessly pacing their Free School classroom. They spat and threatened each other, and they kept howling all the obsessively repetitive obscenities of the jailed. 'Shit man!' 'Fuck you, man!' 'Man, you are a mother-fucking shit man!' Apart from cursing, none of them seemed to have anything to do except when they indulged in an aggressive sort of horse-play sex-play. In this classroom there

96 * what is a menagery?
○ class indistinction

was something dispirited and desperate in the constant outbreaks of sexuality. These all appeared to spring from boredom rather than desire. One was reminded of the way that Eskimos are reputed to make non-stop love in their igloos in order to while away the terrible tedium of their long winter days without light.

The boys would keep coming up behind the girls and lifting up their skirts and goosing them. The girls would scream and giggle. The boys would come up and ram their pelvises against the behinds of the girls. They grabbed them by their hair and pulled their heads back and licked them on the lips. They dragged them down on to the floor and lay on top of them fooling and kissing and tickling. And the girls would scream and giggle. That hideous hyena chorus of hysterical giggling. If so many of the students appeared to be going slightly berserk, if so many students seemed unable to do anything except punch and curse in this classroom, was it because there was clearly no one who could stop all those assaulted girls from giggling? There seemed to be so many of them doing it. Huge fat woman-sized girls wearing skin-tight ribbed sweaters that outlined breasts which had the special provocative pouter-pigeon plumpness of puberty. Beautiful slender girls with proud eyes, dressed in gay chic clothes which they wore with the elegance and arrogance of fashion-models. Tiny, skinny, deprived-looking girls wearing shabby stained jeans and torn tea-shirts. In the rare and blessed moments that the boys gave them the peace to stop giggling they would immediately start doing what they loved doing. They rearranged and decorated each other's hair-styles. It was like hospital occupational-therapy weaving, the way they made braids and then un-picked and re-did them. All their inventiveness seemed to be going into con-structing the most complex and ingenious possible patterns of criss-cross plaiting. They created the most unforgettable Afros. They teased and frothed up each other's hair with huge steel combs until it seemed something much more important than mere hair and became a vast and impenetrable black formation which both crowned them like a halo and dwarfed them by the sheer scale of its contrived gigantism. But just when some girl's style was being completed, when it was being lovingly dotted and adorned with ribbons, seashells, carnations made of scarlet plastic, and a plethora of pretence pearls, the boys would come up and wilfully ruin it. They would snatch away all the seashells, and the plastic flowers and the pearls, and stick them in their own huge black ballooning Afros. Frantic with frustration, the girls screaming and cursing would rush at them and try to strike them in the face with clenched fists. The boys retaliated by grabbing up some of the paintbrushes from the

G

innumerable open pots of housepaint which were lying all over the floor of the classroom, and they completed their vandalism of the girls' creations by splattering their heads with oily pink and yellow emulsion.

All the time that these teenagers were bullying around creating a carnival of cruel chaos in this filthy derelict room, they seemed never to stop eating buns. I had the feeling that I had never been in any interior where so many teenagers were eating quite so many unappetising buns. It almost appeared to be like a regulation that all pupils of this Free School must always be chewing buns, throwing buns, spitting out buns. There were half-bitten buns all over the floor, all over the work-tables. Buns appeared to play an important part in the art that this school produced. There were canvases displayed on the walls on to which the students had sadly glued a few pieces of string, one or two nails and some cardboard coffee-containers. A recurring theme and ingredient ran through all these rather uninspired collages: all of them tended to include in their composition, many, many, lumps of rock-stale, glued-on bun.

The buns at least were concrete, and that I found a relief. For I was still haunted by one vital and missing intangible. Where amongst all the buns and the bull-shitting was the thing which I had come to see? Where, oh where, was the class?

I was starting to feel that I had some kind of fatal blindspot, that I was too close to the class to be able to see it. For although I was unable to perceive the minutest sign of anything which resembled a class, it was only too evident that there were quite a lot of teachers. In this classroom their whiteness made them stand out like the white chalk-marks on their own blackboards. And all these chalky-white teachers were all sitting around and happily talking about the greatness of this class.

They were saying . . . No . . . No one could have conceivably said anything in such a class. They were all screaming in order to get themselves heard above the deafening roar of invective which was surging from the throats of their pupils. They were all screaming how lucky all these kids were to be able to attend this class.

In experiments it has been proved that the human being can become deranged if its ear is over-exposed to too cruel a decibel volume of sound. Suddenly I found myself wondering whether this was what had happened to all these teachers. If after only half an hour I felt already unhinged by the brute noise which seemed to pass through an amplifier as it resounded on the peeling walls of this classroom, what would be the long-term effect on the nervous systems of people who had been conducting these kind of classes day after day for several years? Surely it had to be some sort of derangement induced by noise trauma which was making all these teachers tell me how proud they all were of the look of their classroom. It was only very slowly dawning on me that none of the filthy scrap-heap squalor of this school was the result of miserable necessity. They had told me on my arrival that their school, being one of the new Mini, Open, Free Schools and being considered an exciting, and imaginative, educational project, was very fortunate. Not only was it subsidised by the regular New York State school system, but it had the additional benefit of being heavily endowed with money from private foundations. My initial reaction, as I looked around, was that someone, somewhere, must be absconding with all these funds. But that was before I had realised that all the teachers here considered that the appearance of their classrooms was one of their greatest prides. In this Open, Mini, Free School everything which gave one the feeling that one was in some kind of foul and benighted warehouse had been placed there deliberately to give one that very despairing feeling. At the beginning I had been deeply puzzled as to why the floors of the classrooms were littered with quite such a tangle of unexplained ladders. I had been mystified by all the crusting pots of housepaint, by the non-functional lumps of scrap-iron and concrete, the great stacks of empty beer crates and coca-cola bottles, the piles of ancient sodden newspapers. But now at last it was all becoming clear to me. A deliberately planned show-case of desolation had been thoughtfully constructed in what once must have been a perfectly clean and uncluttered classroom. Its object was to make all these black kids 'learn more'. All the teachers claimed that these kids learned more if they found themselves in the sort of environment to which they were accustomed.

But were all these black kids really accustomed to quite such an environment? However underprivileged their backgrounds, would they normally have great bales of wire, and tangled lumps of scrap-iron, lying around, with quite so many non-purpose pots of paint and ladders, *inside* their houses? It was almost as if all the teachers who ran this school were trying to improve on nature. They had gone so far as to create a classroom in which all the squalor symbols of the used-car lot and the derelict slum street had been surrealistically superimposed on a stage-set decor for a rotting slum interior. Once one accepted that they had done this, one started to feel slightly critical that they had not carried their dream a little further. Why had they neglected to hire some real live winos and junkies to lie around choking and expiring on the

99

floor of the classroom? Why shouldn't the presence of these familiar figures help all these kids to learn even more?

And what for the love of Christ were they all meant to be learning? As an outsider onlooker I couldn't possibly tell, although I had nothing else to do except watch while this charade of a class continued. Was it possible that all these coloured teenagers on the rampage were so perceptive that they could tell?

In the corner a massive handsome Negro boy was teaching another group of boys some dance steps. He was laughing as he fooled around gyrating and wriggling his behind and imitating Mick Jagger. He amused his audience for a while and they copied him. But soon they grew tired of him. They started restlessly shrugging and saying, 'Shit man!' And then the whole group went out of the school and disappeared into the streets.

The teachers were all saying that the kids in this Mini School were the lucky hundred. If they had not been selected to attend this school they would have had to go to one of the ordinary New York public schools. 'How were they selected?' I asked. It appeared that all their names had been written on pieces of paper and they were the fortunate hundred who had been picked out from a hat. One of the teachers said that the great thing about this Mini School was that all the kids here felt that they had *chosen* their own school. I couldn't quite understand why they would feel this, considering they had all been chosen at random like raffle tickets. But in the deafening nerve-drilling din of the classroom nothing seemed more tiring and unrewarding than to try to quibble.

'Would it be easier to talk if we went out into the corridor?' I asked. If they wanted to explain the strengths and merits of their class I felt that anywhere would be more tolerable than to remain in their classroom where, although they were all shouting at full lungs' bellow, it was often only possible to pick up the tail-end of any sentence.

'Does our chaos really bother you so much?' They were smiling pityingly. Suddenly I was being condescended to. I was being made to feel I was like the person who wants to make an omelette without breaking eggs, or the amateur visitor to the surgery who faints at the very first sign of blood.

'This class is like a three-ring circus,' they told me proudly. 'Something different is always going on in every corner. Everywhere you look someone is always doing something different, someone is having a fight, someone is making love, someone is doing a sum. That's what all these black kids like. They like variety. They like the class to be lively. They learn better if the class is

100

lively. It's like you find you learn better if you are on the subway in the rush-hour. You just cut yourself off from it all and learn.'

It was slightly quieter when we all went out for a moment into the corridor. There was only the scream and jostle of all the groups of teenage Negroes who were leaving. All the time a really tremendous amount of pupils seemed to be leaving. But after about half an hour some of them would suddenly reappear for no apparent reason. When they reappeared they would just sit around on the work-benches and they were much quieter. It seemed to me that quite a lot of them were most distinctly stoned.

If, as there appeared to be quite good reason to suspect, a large percentage of these kids spent most of their schooldays shooting heroin on the streets, one wondered who there was to care. One had the feeling that all their teachers had reached a despairing point where they were beyond caring. Exhausted, avant-garde, and idealistic, their teachers had been forced to retreat into an isolated and ivory-tower position. And by now it was only by dint of this lofty and blinkered position that any of them were able to go on conducting this black travesty of a class.

And yet the more I talked to them, the more I found myself acquiring a perverse admiration and fondness for all these friendly teachers. Underpaid and over-conscientious, they unselfishly dragged themselves to this hideous classroom every morning. Every day they stuck it out. Uncorrupt, and uncomplaining, they sat around in their bun-littered, urine-splashed Open School, and ignored and endured the open contempt of their pupils.

Far too innocent and engaged to be aware of any irony, they had pinned up posters with pious words on the walls of their classroom. 'Children are the world's most valuable resource and its best hope for the future.' 'Consistency is the last refuge of the unimaginative.' And these last words made me think once again of the tongue-twister, 'Imagine an unimaginative menagery manager unimaginatively managing an unimaginative menagery.'

Saintly visionaries, all these Open School teachers seemed to be able to see good in everything. I asked them if they had many Mini-school pupils who never troubled to turn up at the Mini School at all. They said that the level of absenteeism was very high but there was nothing anyone could do about it. They added that when the student attendance was very poor it could sometimes be quite a good thing for they tended to have a somewhat better class. The class . . . the class . . . There was something mystical in the way they always managed to keep on talking about the class.

When a little gang of boys started pointlessly hurling paper plates at them,

101

it clearly pleased them. 'They are making flying saucers!' It took me quite a while to realise why they were so delighted. When these teenagers made their flying saucers their teachers could somehow persuade themselves that it betokened some kind of a blossoming interest in science.

'All these black kids feel like kings,' they kept telling me. 'In this school all these kids know that no one is ever going to order them around. They know that this is the place where no one is ever going to try to make them do anything they don't want to do. It's a new feeling for them. It makes them all feel like emperors.'

When we went back into the classroom I looked at all the desperate and disgruntled black faces of the students. They were still all snarling around tormenting each other and shouting 'Shit' just as they had been all morning. But now I tried to see them in a new way. I tried to see them all as emperors – emperors who were all attending their emperor's new class.

'What class is this?' I hoped I was not being offensive and I was relieved that everyone seemed to find it normal that at some point I would find it necessary to ask the question. 'It's History,' I was told. 'Tomorrow is English.'

'History' consisted of a game being brought out and placed on one of the work-tables. Different-coloured counters were distributed among four fourteen-year old boys. The red counter represented Russia, the blue one France, the green one Germany, etc. A fight broke out immediately for all of them wanted to be Russia. 'I'm Russia!' 'No, I'm Russia!' They punched and wrestled and cursed as they tried to grab hold of the red counter. The teachers patiently waited until the most massive and thuggish-looking of the boys predictably won the fight and they told him he was to be Russia.

The game had a board on which was printed a map of the world. It appeared that you were meant to move the counters around the board in turns and various countries could invade other countries. The only trouble was that none of the four players seemed to agree on the rules. Almost immediately they were all waving clenched fists and pounding on the work-table, their faces contorted with fury. 'He just already went. Damn him!' One of the boys kept screaming. 'He's just went again and he's just already went! Shitty cheater!'

History was turning into pandemonium and the teachers watched and smiled benignly. 'Now they are learning what international politics is all about!' someone said with satisfaction. 'They all feel like kings,' a pleasant little white woman murmured with what was horribly like a happy sigh.

The board of 'History' was sent flying with all its counters. The players seemed to be in such a state of uncontrolled fury with each other that an onlooker could only pray that none of them were carrying knives. But after a lot of shadow-boxing and howling description of what they would like to do to each other, their own fight fortunately seemed suddenly to bore them. And still complaining that Germany had taken Russia's fucking turn, all four left the school together to fight it out, or forget their History lesson on the streets.

'How often does someone get badly hurt in these kind of fights?' I asked. 'Not as often as you would think. It happens, of course. I mean it just has to happen. But we don't get half the fatal fights that they get in the regular schools. You would think we would. But we don't. That's just the way it is.'

The 'History class' was still going on. It now took the form of the two white teachers quietly playing the same game together in a corner. They hoped to attract new players but their class did not seem to be in the least interested in History. No one went near them. There was no one who wanted to watch them. So they had to carry on regardless. And together they just went on playing, on and on.

While 'History' was going on I listened to two girls who were chatting together about something which obviously concerned them far more than History—abortion. 'No one's going to make me have no abortion. You know what they do to you with abortion? They just take a knife and they just split you down the front. I'd rather have the baby and flush it down the toilet.'

'I hope you can come tomorrow,' someone was saying to me. 'Tomorrow is English and we have a Puerto Rican poet coming to take it. Tomorrow there ought to be a very good class.'

'What is he going to do in English tomorrow?' I asked.

'You never know what he is going to do. He always makes the class very varied. Sometimes he reads to the kids. Sometimes he has Discussion.'

'What does he read when he reads?' I asked. No one seemed to know quite. I could understand only too well why no one was too certain what the poet read although they must all have seen him doing it innumerable times. For if one was to assume that 'English' would tend to be very much like 'History' anyone who tried to read in it would have to be resigned to being seen and not heard.

A teacher with an eighteenth-century pirate's hair-style and an immense crucifix round his neck started talking. 'A few years ago we would have only given all these kids black stuff. But now we don't believe they have to have that. Why should we limit them? Right? So we give them quite a lot of white stuff. And they respond to it pretty well. We give them things like Jack London.'

While he was talking I started to have the most horrible hallucination. In my hideous vision I thought I could actually *see* the Puerto Rican poet reading. I could see him tucked away in the corner of the classroom. And there he was reading with a heavy Spanish accent. He was just reading, and reading, and reading, Jack London. And none of his students gave a sign that they had noticed that he was reading. And the poet was so engrossed with his own reading that he hardly seemed to be aware of all the non-fatal and the fatal fights which were raging around him. He completely ignored the pregnant fourteen-year-old girls with their pearl-encrusted Afro hairstyles who were all singing in a chorus that they would rather have the baby and flush it down the toilet.

'Don't you want to come and take a look at Remedial Reading?' someone was asking me. I felt so tired and depressed and dizzy.

In New York, in a city which feels itself to be in a state of crisis, all its inhabitants are so terrorised and obsessed by street muggers, for the last week I had been listening to different kinds of New Yorkers all suggesting different solutions to the problem of muggers. 'I warn you, here in New York now we just talk about two things : money, and muggers. Don't try to talk to us about Vietnam. Please don't try to talk to us about *anything* except money and muggers. We just won't be interested.'

'Don't you realise that none of us dare go down the block to the super-market without taking ten dollars to give to the muggers when they mug us? How can anyone live like that? It's like a street tax. Who can afford that? No wonder we all talk about nothing but money. And even if you give the muggers your ten dollars there's no guarantee that they'll think it's enough. And then they may be muggers who are just doing it for kicks. So you'll lose your ten dollars and you'll end up with a knife jabbed through your spine anyway.'

Although it seemed to be generally agreed that New York muggers could often in practice be white, in popular white imagination they were generally seen to be black. 'Only machine-guns will ever make the New York streets safe for anyone to walk in. You are just going to have to go right in there with guns and get all those black bastards off the streets. No one can go on like this. Someone is going to have to do something. Someone is going to have to clean this city up !'

'You will never stop the mugging unless you do something about educating the blacks. No one wants to face it but they've got to spend the hell of a lot more money on education for the blacks. Someone has got to provide some kind of imaginative black re-education. If this city doesn't want to end up with mass genocide – black education is the only hope.'

Sitting watching 'History' in this Free School I kept thinking about the white liberals who thought that black education was the answer to the city's problems. I wondered if they would count this 'History' class as education – if they would want to spend more money on giving all these black teenagers even more of this kind of class.

All the teachers said that they thought there was quite a good hope that eventually all the schools for blacks in the entire United States would be 'Open' and 'Free'. I found myself marvelling at the teachers. How could they have ever had the nerve to tell me that they found the presence of more than one onlooker tended to disturb their class? It was only too painfully obvious that just because I was white, and just because I was wandering aimlessly round the classroom, looking fatigued and rather desperate, all the pupils in this Free School assumed – not only that I was a teacher – but that I was a teacher who was in the actual act of teaching. None of them gave the slightest sign that they found this in any way interesting or disturbing. If I wanted happily to carry on with my teaching, there was nothing in this School to make them feel it in any way concerned them.

If I had brought twenty strange white people to this classroom, and we had all milled around benignly in the confusion, it was most unlikely that any of the students would have felt that our presence in any way affected them. They would have vaguely registered that quite a lot of white people seemed to have turned up that day. With understandable contempt and indifference, they would have assumed that if all these extra white people had appeared – by the very whiteness of their nature – all these people must be teaching. The condescension of their attitude would have been very similar to that of their teachers when they assumed that any black person who happened to drop in for a few minutes to meet their friends in Open House style, to an Open School class, was automatically 'learning'.

I wondered if any of the Negro leaders ever attended these Open School classes. What would a Negro leader feel if he was to sit in on a class similar to 'History'? Was it possible that he would feel that I was biased and blind to all the good that this Free School was doing all these black children, that I was ignorant of the true problems and therefore over-critical and unfair?

Could he take the view that all these Negro teenagers were ineducable so that it made little difference if their schools were conducted like 'three-ring circuses', for at least this kind of schooling put so little pressure on them that it made them feel like kings which was all they should expect?

I was wondering if anyone from the New York foundations that endowed this Open School with private funds ever came to see what it was like in operation. Was an Open School something which could only be promising and imaginative if it remained where it should always remain, as a bright-sounding idea on paper? How many of the Free School pupils really gained from the total lack of structure and order in their classes? How many found there was all that much creative freedom in being part of a class in which everyone was encouraged to do their 'own thing'? In escaping the tyranny of dull traditional disciplined education had all these black students not simply become victims of another equally oppressive tyranny — the tyranny of their own aimlessness and anarchy?

'Don't you want to take a look at "Remedial Reading"?' someone kept on asking me. By now I felt that the very last thing that I would want to see in the world would be 'Remedial Reading'. Just as I feared I could imagine 'English' so I feared I could imagine 'Remedial Reading'. I had an instant vision that it would be another dirty room in which a tense little well-meaning white woman would be sitting in the midst of her black chaos with her 'method' and a tremendous lot of reading charts. I dreaded seeing her with her charts. I dreaded seeing her being so proud of her charts. But off I went escorted by a group of friendly teachers to 'Remedial Reading' which was in a different building, in a different block.

And there she was, just as I had feared she would be. Against the blackness of her class she looked so pale she almost appeared to be transparent. Only one thing about her surprised me. Never in the wildest stretches of my paranoid imagination had I ever visualised her as having quite so many reading charts.

The walls of her classroom were ablaze with multi-coloured lettering. Her alphabets were plastered everywhere and they looked like glittering mosaics. They brightened the whole room with their splendid splash of psychedelic colour.

Her magnificent charts, unfortunately, seemed to be infinitely gayer and more encouraging than her situation. For her students' lack of interest in her charts appeared to be identical to the lack of interest I had just seen displayed towards 'History'. Her classroom was in a state of almost epic disorder, and

106

there she was, gallantly bobbing around like a little white cork in a black seething antagonistic sea of Afro hair-styles.

All the pupils in 'Remedial Reading' appeared to be much larger than any of the students that I had seen in 'History'. Maybe they only seemed to be larger because one knew that they had to be totally illiterate to be in this classroom, and somehow this very fact enlarged them. And when they all kept fooling around in an infantilistic frenzy, screaming and teasing, giggling and making love, it was all the more disturbing because they looked like fully-grown adults. Also the classroom of 'Remedial Reading' was much smaller than that of 'History' and less equipped to absorb so many very large students who were all so desperately doing their 'own thing'.

The teacher tried to tell me about her reading method. 'I use the Cattegno method,' she shouted. But it was no use. When she tried to tell me more I couldn't hear her. I could just see that her lips were moving and that she was pointing with her ruler at all her coloured alphabets. She realised that in the conditions that prevailed in her classroom she could never succeed in making me understand her method. She shrugged sadly and then she gave up. She came over to me and bellowed in my ear, 'I guess when you think about it – the method isn't all that important. I guess the only real method is to take advantage of the moment. I guess that if you really think about it – the method is really in you.'

It was lunch-time. The classroom suddenly thinned and one understood why everyone who worked in this school seemed to feel that a high level of student absenteeism made for a better class.

I sat at a table and ate hot-dogs with the teachers. They all spoke of the poor black kids who were still being sent to regular New York schools; they spoke with so much horror that they might just as well have been referring to gas-chambers. They were so persuasive that I soon found myself infected by their hatred of the regular New York schools. I felt that I would be too cowardly and squeamish even to dare to take a look at them. I just took it on faith that they must all be immeasurably more horrifying than this Mini, Free School. I thought of the classroom of 'History' and I thought of 'Remedial Reading' and tried to visualise something a billion times worse. Just as it is difficult truly to visualise the pure and perfect Heaven – so imagination can sometimes prove too feeble to properly visualise the really pure and perfect Hell.

BURNS UNIT

'At least you are lucky to live so near the best burns hospital in the world . . .
The new techniques are staggering. East Grinstead is still farther ahead
than the United States and Russia. McIndoe got his start in the war. His
hospital was near the aerodromes. He got all the burnt war pilots . . .'

As a visitor it was the afternoons which always seemed the worst inside the
sealed-off, germ-free, centre section of the Queen Victoria Burns Unit. There
was an eerie timelessness to their hush and their languor. The burned would
be there so very still inside their isolated and tropically-heated glass cubicles
like dogs napping in some invisible sun. In the afternoons all the corridors were
deserted and desolate, their silence only sometimes broken by the sound of
some nurse's sterile blue plastic galoshes, which would make a squish as if she
was ploughing through winter leaves. One kept expecting these hospital
passages to smell of antiseptic, but instead they smelt unpleasantly of nothing.
The air had a curious heavy lifelessness. Sometimes one felt its very sterility
could choke one, and realised that one missed the presence of germs.

They were far too still, those afternoons with all the patients lying there
under their afternoon sedation, with their burns drying out in the artificial
heat like washing in a boiler-room. One started to feel submerged as if one
were on a submarine missing anything that could call to mind life on land.
One kept hoping that it would soon be a meal-time so that at least one would
hear the commonplace clank of the huge steel sterilising container from which
the patients were distributed their surgical-gauze-like hospital food. One
missed the purposeful bustle of all the white-masked specialists and surgeons
who only visited and did the grafts and operations in the mornings. One
missed anything which could break the germ-free Unit's oppressive afternoon
atmosphere of motionless and patient waiting – anything which could stop one
feeling that the main activity in this Unit was waiting – waiting to be better –
waiting to be dead.

At the main-desk in the afternoons, the on-duty head-nurse would be sitting slumped over her evening newspaper. Behind her there stood the great huddle of silent television sets which relayed the pictures of all the patients who were on the danger list. The cameras above their beds photographed them from odd and aerial angles, and their images as they appeared on the screens looked weird and fragmented. Where was the familiar crackling chatter of news commentators? Where were all the usual panel games and the breezy flashing faces of pop-singers? One felt disoriented and disturbed seeing only so many never-changing, soundless images of burn-blotched stomachs and strapped-apart thighs in close-up. There was something grisly about the way the cameras kept such stubborn focus on so many disembodied genitals all pierced with the essential badge of the burnt, the catheter.

'You will get used to it all,' they said. But I never did. When my daughter was on television I never got used to seeing her there. One day she appeared simultaneously on three different sets. None of the three hers quite seemed to be her. All the same I often found myself leaving the real her who was lying unconscious in her cubicle, in order to go out into the corridor to look at them. Hour after hour there was often nothing to do inside the germ-free Unit and I kept staring at these screens as if, by association, I expected them to act as some kind of distraction. And sometimes I found that if I stared at them long enough I could start to have the insane illusion that if someone was to unplug all these television sets, her illness would disappear with her image.

'You will get used to it all . . .' But I never got used to the way that all the patients in this hospital were laid out on display like exhibits, that they could all be viewed from an outer 'polluted' corridor which was arranged like the reptile house at the zoo. As you passed glass window after glass window, each room seemed like a glass cage showing a different tropically heated and brilliantly lit specimen. Were they all beyond caring that they were so exposed to the morbid curiosity of the most casual of passers-by? Stripped by necessity of even a sheet to cover their nakedness, was there some good scientific reason why they should be so totally stripped of privacy? There they all lay like Francis Bacon figures framed in their dehumanised postures with black charred legs strapped apart and their genitals pierced by their catheters. There were women whose breasts were blown up like balloons in two giant vermilion blisters. There were infants in cots, tiny pieces of purple zebra flesh, their only clothing the bandages that covered a recent graft wound. There were faceless men lying there with pipes which were feeding something vital into something scarlet which must have once been a nose. Sometimes one of the glass display rooms would suddenly be empty and one would see only the narrow surgical

109

bed with its brilliant orange rubber anti-sticking burn pad. And as in a reptile cage which at first sight seems to contain nothing, one would start to feel that some living creature must still really be lurking on that flaming pad, that it was invisible only because it was so well camouflaged by its natural surroundings.

On certain days as one walked down the outer corridor one would see a brightly lit tableau of doctors and nurses keeping a tense round-the-clock vigil about a bed. Hour after hour they would hardly move. Their arms were lifted as they supported their huge bottles of blood, saline and plasma, and they looked as if they were holding them up on high like chalices. All day and all night they fingered the tubes of the drips as if they were rosaries. Was it possible that they could save that pulpy object? Did one hope that that pulpy black object in its coma could be saved? Did they all know it was beyond salvation and yet still feel bound to give it the respect of some kind of public and scientific last rites? Was it out of respect for it, or for their own techniques, that they refused to pull down the blinds?

No visitors were ever allowed inside the sealed-off centre germ-free section of the Burns Unit. This rule was observed with severity, but it was relaxed for the mothers of child-patients. Inside the Unit the mothers were the most feared and despised minority. They were regarded rather in the way that some British people regard Uganda Asians, as a race of interloping undesirables who had somehow managed to insinuate their way into the country by craftily acquiring a bogus passport. Although the mothers wore the identical regulation white gowns and caps and masks and galoshes as the hospital workers, never for a moment were they made to feel that anyone was fooled by their external trappings. As a Belfast Protestant claims he can spot a Belfast Catholic walking in any crowded thoroughfare, so a mother could instantly be spotted among all the other white-clad figures who thronged the hospital corridors. Once detected, the mothers always aroused a frisson of fear, and hostility, for they were all known to be Typhoid Marys. They were carriers of foreign bodies that were deeply threatening and unwelcome to the Unit. Into this impersonal and functional sealed-off world of science they brought their total uselessness; they brought personal panic, anguish and hysteria, and most dreaded of all they brought squeamishness and germs. With their undesirable qualities oozing from every pore, the mothers would go flitting around the unpolluted passages with their deranged eyes peering over their masks as they tried to get some kind of a prognosis from hospital personnel passing by, who very much resented being waylaid and pestered because they were all passing with some vital purpose.

110

'Will they be able to save his sight, Sister?'

'Will she have to have very many more grafts?'

'That, I'm afraid, you will have to ask the doctor . . .'

'I'm very sorry but I really can't give you an answer. I suggest you ask the doctor.'

And everyone knew that it was impossible to ask the doctor for, whoever he was, he was unavailable. If ever you found a doctor he always turned out to be an under-doctor and he would suggest you refer your questions to some higher and absent doctor. One day as I was walking down the corridors of the Unit I was certain that I had found *the* doctor. He was very old with bushy eyebrows which looked even whiter than his surgeon's cap. He walked with a stoop, but there was immense pride and authority in his slow plod. His intelligent exhausted eyes looked worn-out and black-ringed from sleepless vigils. He was frowning and preoccupied and his handsome craggy face appeared to have been prematurely aged by the grinding responsibility of his daily life-and-death decisions. McIndoe must have once walked the wards of the Burns Unit with the same confident dignity. Now that McIndoe was dead, this distinguished old surgeon must surely be the man of supreme authority and genius in this hospital. I stopped him and asked how my daughter was progressing. Over his surgical mask his exhausted old eyes stared at me astounded. I realised that he didn't speak English. Later I saw him walking with the same proud and dignified plod carrying a mop and a pail. Finally it became clear that he was the man who was employed to clean the nurses' lavatories.

'You will get used to it all . . .'

But I never got used to the way that once the mothers had been swabbed and dressed up like medical extras in a television hospital comedy they lost all individual identity. Once they were admitted into the sterile section it was as if they shared a single code number and were all referred to very simply as 'the mother'. Inside the suffocating highly-heated cubicle the child whose body was the colour of blackened bacon would be screaming for water with the terrible delirious thirst of the newly burned.

'Tell the mother to tell the little girl that she can't possibly have any water. She's having all that she's allowed through the drip in her hand.'

'Get me some water! Get me some water!' And then, as if she had remembered being told that you only get what you want if you ask politely, the child would start whispering.

'Please may I have just one little sip of water. Please. Please. Just one little tiny sip . . .'

'Tell the mother to tell the little girl that she can have one teaspoon of water in two hours time. And tell the mother to tell the little girl that it's no use her making such a racket. She's got to wait two hours.' And then a little later . . .

'Tell the mother that all she's doing is upsetting the child. Could you tell the mother it would be really much better if she were to leave . . .'

And then, out of the stifling cubicle, and into the corridor, where all the other screams which were coming from all the other glass cubicles were relayed on an amplifying system. Why did they have to turn the amplifiers up so loud? Was there some good medical reason which would justify it? All the screams seemed to be only too audible without this kind of magnification. You could feel you might go berserk in these corridors where such a hideous chorus of pain-screams were piped like music. And yet it was obvious that apart from the visitor-mothers no one in this closed medical community was in the least disturbed by it. How long would one have to stay inside the Burns Unit to become immune to this chilling broadcast of howls? Would one ever learn to ignore it as one learns barely to hear canned music?

'McIndoe had the magic touch,' someone told me.

'McIndoe could go in to see a woman who would never again be able to speak except through a plastic tube in her cheek and when he left her she felt like a queen . . .'

McIndoe's legend was so alive inside the Burns Unit that it was with a feeling of grief and almost grievance that you realised that, when you sat with his plaster bust in the waiting-room, that was the closest you could ever get to meeting him. Every day there were so many hours of waiting while, over-life-size, and up on his pedestal, McIndoe never stopped smiling. He looked so strong and capable in his surgeon's cap. There was something comforting and all-knowing in his smile. If there were no other visitors in the waiting-room one sometimes felt tempted to start asking him questions. He at least was pinnioned there in his plaster. In the Unit that he had created he seemed the only medical figure who was unable to shake you off and hurry away. McIndoe must surely know the prognosis for every single patient that was lying there so raw and naked in those germ-free box-rooms. They must all be doing very well. He seemed so obviously delighted with their progress. The prognosis for all of them had to be excellent, even for that new man who had just been brought in from a chemical explosion. For why else would McIndoe be smiling?

And then staring up at him one could sometimes imagine that something less consoling was creeping into his smile, some touch of Olympian and scientific ruthlessness, some touch of the greed of the genius.

'McIndoe got all the burnt war pilots . . .' For a moment one could start to see him like a farmer praying for rain. Then a deluge of charred guinea-pigs showering down on the Tudor motels of East Grinstead from the sky . . . Convoys of ambulances sirening through the black-out. The germ-free units mushrooming with saline plants, plasma-drips, body suspension belts, 'blue rooms' with the sterilising 'blue light'. And McIndoe smiling, seeing supply meet demand.

On the day that my daughter was to be discharged from the Burns Unit I sat for the last time in the visitors' waiting-room with McIndoe. As I looked at the face of this perennially smiling plastic surgeon I could imagine that yet another element was creeping into his plaster expression, a certain dread, a nervousness, an edgy fear that I might try to express my gratitude. Long-dead, and perched high, and preserved as the hospital's idol, McIndoe still seemed alive enough to fear that, in all the weeks I had spent in his Unit, I had grasped almost nothing of his values. All that he seemed to be praying was that I would not disappoint him by showing that I had still failed to understand that he would be bound to feel the same contempt for gratitude that he felt for all the other gratuitous emotions which were in no way allied to effective action. To him any graft was more valuable than any amount of gratitude. He saw sympathy as a very wretched substitute for skill. He saw precision and plasma as incomparably superior to compassion.

As I left the waiting-room I looked back at McIndoe, and his statue face now suddenly seemed to be amused at the idea that visitors to his Unit could ever expect to find their visits enjoyable. Clearly he was only too aware they would be bound to feel that there was something inhuman in the machine-like, skilled routines, in the apparent immunity to suffering, of his team of white-coated workers in this sterile medical compound. But this could concern him very little because he knew so well how the burnt became different. They learnt that even the coldest and most impersonal curative action was less inhuman than sentimental and empathising inaction. McIndoe had seen the way they would refuse to be discharged from the Burns Unit when there was no longer any medical reason for them to stay on there, for what they feared was not the callous impersonality of this aquarium-like scientific depot. Their terror was the outside world where they knew they would be treated with something which would be inconceivable within the Unit, the twin cruelties of pity and horror.

H

Ulster

NEVER BREATHE A WORD

We only ever knew him as McAfee. The harness-room had no electricity, and only a crack of a window, and when it rained he often spent the whole day in its darkness. He would crouch there on a low stool, polishing up a stirrup, rubbing yellow soap into a saddle, and he always seemed more like an animal than a man, and he made the harness-room seem like his lair. My sister and I liked him rather as we liked hunting, and halters, and snaffles – only because he was to do with the horse.

Every morning he would arrive on his bicycle to take us out riding, and we would go out jogging along behind his huge bay mare, two plump little girls in cork-lined velvet riding-caps, on two plump little barrel-bellied ponies. McAfee spoke very little on these rides, and when he did it was difficult to understand him. He had a rasping Ulster accent and he had lost every tooth in his mouth, and although he owned a brilliant pair of over-white and over-even dentures, he refused to wear them except for 'special occasions' – when he took us to horse-shows or out hunting.

He chain-smoked as he rode, holding his cigarette between his dark, lumpy gums, and when he went over a jump he never lost it. 'You're alright!' he always shouted automatically whenever we fell trying to follow him over stone-walls and ditches. Perdita once broke her collar-bone and never dared mention it to anyone when she got home. 'You just never breathe a word,' McAfee told her. 'I don't like people who are over-fussy.'

He had once been a professional jockey and one of his own shoulders had been broken so often in racing falls that it had become deformed. His right arm was far shorter than his left, and it dangled down uselessly from a hump. Yet when he was riding, he made the peculiar way that he sat so crookedly in a short-stirruped jockey's crouch, holding both his reins in his left hand, seem correct, like some superior technique. It was only when he dismounted that it was always shocking to see that he was not much taller than we were. The moment that he got down from his mare he looked as though half of his body had suddenly been amputated, and one saw that he had the over-large

117

head and torso and the diminished child's legs of a dwarf. He waddled from top-heaviness when he walked. The way he always kept his bandy little spindle-legs in their riding breeches and boots so very far apart made them look as though they were perpetually gripping the flanks of some invisible horse.

At that time Perdita and I loved horses with a single-minded and sentimental passion. We would talk for hours about their different characters, be worried that we had hurt their feelings. We loved the smell of their sweat, the spikiness of their eyelashes, the velvet feel of their noses. McAfee always made it very plain that he found our attitude extremely silly and irritating. To him a horse was as functional as a tractor, and he wanted it correctly used in order to get the most out of it. 'Jag her mouth!' he would shout at us if our ponies reared. We were always too scared and he was always cantankerous and scornful. 'You should have jagged her mouth, and brought her down over herself, and then jumped yourself clear. You should have learned her . . .'

'Couldn't you break a horse's spine doing that?'

'If you're so feared to take a risk, Caroline – you'll have all your money, but you'll never do a thing with a horse.'

McAfee had ten children, and his house was five miles from ours, and sometimes when we passed it on our rides, they would all come out into the chicken-yard to wave. Occasionally Mrs McAfee came out, a thin, exhausted-looking woman with mole-grey marks under her eyes. She was usually holding some half-naked and bawling baby. McAfee's children would gape at us with respect and curiosity because of our ponies, and Perdita and I would gape back with respect and curiosity because the McAfees were so many – and because they looked so muddy and so poor.

The way that McAfee sometimes spoke of his old racing days made us realise that he felt that there was a sadness and a disgrace to the fact that he had ended up his life as a children's groom. He only ever seemed happy when he was telling us some of his old racing tricks – showing us how he used to press up his foot under another passing jockey's stirrup so that he would lose his balance and fall. 'And nothing could ever be proved!' McAfee's grin would show all his empty gums.

One day we were going down a lane and McAfee suddenly reined back his mare in order to ride alongside my pony.

'How would you like to be the best wee rider in the whole of Ireland?'

I thought he was taunting me. I found it very dispiriting, but I knew only too well that McAfee thought that I would always be a hopeless rider – that

118

I had bad hands – no natural seat – very little control – and I rarely used my knees. Often when we went out hunting McAfee had told me that he was ashamed that all the other grooms should see him with me. 'With all of them looking at you, Caroline – I would have really hoped that you wouldn't have made such an exhibition . . . It breaks my heart that you couldn't have done better than that.'

But now McAfee was whispering as though it was a secret. 'I would like to see you the best rider in the whole of Ireland.'

I shrugged as though the idea bored me. I wished he would change the subject. It seemed pointless and painful to talk pipe-dreams.

'How do you think that all the really big people in the horse world do it?' I couldn't understand why McAfee kept on whispering.

'How do you think that they manage to be always up there with the hounds at all the hunts – to go round all the shows carrying off all the cups? Why do you think that the walls of their stables are red with rosettes? Take a big woman like Lady Mary Berry – how do you think she does it?'

I thought of Lady Mary Berry. I had seen her at all the horse-shows, fat-faced and formidable, in her bowler and her impeccably shined boots, coolly taking perfect double-banks – the crowds all clapping . . .

'How does she do it?'

McAfee leaned down over the side of his mare's neck and whispered to me through his gums : 'Pills.'

'Pills?'

'All the big winners – they all do it the same way. There's only one reason why they manage to carry off all the competitions at the Balmoral – and the Dublin – and all the important shows over in England. They all take the pills.'

'How can pills make you a good rider?' I felt slow-witted, but I just couldn't understand.

McAfee seemed to be rather flustered as though he hadn't expected the question. He thought for a while, and then he suddenly said, 'Hands!' And I wondered why he seemed so pleased with his answer.

'Without good hands – you'll never be a rider!' McAfee's mare reared and whinnied as he cracked down his bone-handled crop on her haunches to emphasise his point. 'It's been that way since the beginning of time. You've got to have the feel of a horse's mouth. No one's ever made a name for themselves in the horse world unless they've taken the pills for their hands.'

'Do you take the pills?' If McAfee took the pills, I was wondering why he wasn't more internationally famous as a horseman.

'I always used to take them in my time. I couldn't have raced without them. I haven't taken them lately . . .' His voice sounded suddenly depressed. 'Now I don't have much occasion.'

When we got back to the stables McAfee helped me dismount from my pony. 'You think it over, Caroline. It's a terrible thing to see you riding the way you do. You never breathe a word to a soul and I'll be seeing what I can do for you.'

All that night I felt vaguely disturbed and tempted by the idea of McAfee's pills.

A week later we were going through a bridle-path in some woods and McAfee suddenly said, 'I've got them!'

'Got what?'

'I've got hold of some of those pills.'

'Where did you get them?'

'I went round to the stables at Mount Stewart and bought a bottle from Lady Mary Berry's groom.' He gave one of his crafty gummy grins.

'Can I see them?'

'I wouldn't dare to give them to you in the daylight. At first Lady Mary's groom didn't even want to sell them to me. They are very hard to get. They are as precious as gold. He made me pay the earth for them. He says that everyone in Ulster is after them. Once people know that you've got them – they always manage to steal them away from you. I promised him that I wouldn't hand them over to you in a place where anyone might see.'

'But who on earth could see here?' We were so far from anyone, with about two miles of dense trees and scrubby undergrowth separating us from the nearest house.

McAfee rolled his eyes and his manure-clogged fingernail pointed in a paranoid way at the trunks of various beeches and oaks. 'How do you ever know who might be watching you?'

He looked suspiciously at the plump little form of my sister with her pig-tails and her black velvet cap as she jogged along on her lazy pony slushing through the winter leaves. 'How do you ever know who you can trust?'

We came to a clearing encircled by dripping laurel bushes. 'You better meet me right here in this spot tonight, Caroline. You know how to get here. But you've got to wait until it's dark. Daylight's not safe. And don't let people see you setting off. They might guess where you're going and follow you. Once it gets dark I'll be waiting for you here – and then I'll give you the pills.'

Once it got dark I had not the very faintest desire to have the pills. I didn't even believe that they would work on me, though I imagined that McAfee of all people should know what he was talking about if it was to do with riding. In any case even if the pills were as good as he claimed I only wanted to stay in the nursery and toast bread on a fork on its wood fire – to read comics in the warmth and the light in my dressing-gown – listen to a serial on the radio. The idea of bicycling off alone in the dark to that dank, dismal clearing in the woods terrified me. I decided that I wouldn't go.

But then I kept on thinking of poor McAfee waiting, and waiting. I was frightened that he might wait for me there all night in the wet and the cold and by morning he would be so furious that I didn't see that I would ever dare to go riding with him again. I only wished to God that I had never let him think that I wanted to take his pills. I couldn't even remember that I had ever actually told him that I was interested in taking them – but somehow he had just assumed it because he knew that I secretly wanted to be the best rider in Ireland. I couldn't stop thinking how hurt and disappointed he would be if I just let him wait out there in the woods and never turned up. He cared so much about making me a really good rider. He had taken so much trouble to get hold of the pills for me, and they had cost him so much money.

I went out to the shed and got out my bicycle. There was no moon that night and it was drizzling. I felt a terror and a desperation as I peddled off, wobbling along in the muddy ruts of wheel tracks. At that time I had a horror of the dark and could only ever sleep if my bedroom was a blaze of night-lights. I didn't dare look to the right or the left. On either side of me the darkness seemed like an evil, inky soup, floating with every ghastly kind of supernatural spook and spectre. I tried to concentrate on the weak, swaying light thrown by my bicycle lamp. When I got up to the woods, I found it even worse. My tyres made the crackle of footsteps as they ground the rotting beech-nuts. Every branch seemed like the grabbing arm of some insane old woman strangler.

Finally I got to the clearing and I saw that there was no one there, and suddenly I detested McAfee. He had made all this peculiar fuss about meeting me up here in the woods – and then he hadn't even bothered to come. He had made me make this loathesome, lonely ride in the dark for nothing.

And then suddenly something rustled in one of the laurel bushes, and somehow I knew it was McAfee. But why was he crouching in the middle of a soaking bush? He had known I was coming – so why was he hiding?

121

Out he came from the laurel leaves with an odd little hop like a rabbit. Seeing the shadow form of his stunted legs and his hump, I thought of Rumplestiltskin. When he turned on a torch I saw that he was not wearing the old tweed cap that he always wore in the daytime. He was wearing his best shiny bowler, the one he only ever wore when he went out hunting. And I didn't know why it chilled me so much to see that he was suddenly wearing his false teeth.

He just stood there staring at me. I felt that he was frightened of something and couldn't understand what he could be so frightened of. I had never seen him show any fear before, he had always seemed like a man without a nerve in his body when he was riding. And all the light from his torch seemed to be reflected in his teeth . . . They looked dazzling as though they were painted with phosphorus – they were the only glowing thing in this hideous winter wood.

'Have you brought the pills?' I didn't want the pills. I just wanted him to say something – anything – to stop silently standing there on his bandy little booted legs, looking so foolish in his bowler.

He seemed to be unable to speak. He made some odd, fish-like sucking movements with his mouth, and it was as though he was so unused to wearing his teeth that he was gagged by them.

I started to get back on to my bicycle. I wanted to get away from him. It seemed to me that McAfee had gone mad staring at me in this peculiar, wary way as though he didn't dare take his eyes off me for fear I might suddenly attack him.

'You mustn't go!' His voice came through his dentures with a whistle. He fumbled in the pocket of his jacket and then handed me a grubby little glass bottle full of pills.

'Swallow them down, Caroline – they'll do you a lot of good. You'll be sorry for ever if you don't take them.'

I looked suspiciously at the bottle. I didn't like the look of these scruffy little white pills.

'What are they?'

I saw that there had once been some writing on the label of the bottle, but it was now unreadable because someone had scratched it off with the point of a knife.

'No one quite knows what they are. But it doesn't matter – they do wonders for everyone. You be a good wee girl. You just swallow them down.'

'Why has the writing on the label been scratched off?'

McAfee suddenly flinched back, rolling his eyes as though I had struck him in the face.

'I didn't do it.'

'Who did it?'

'The bottle was like that when they gave it to me.'

'I don't want to take them unless I know what they are.'

'That's right. I think that you are quite right.' He almost seemed relieved, as though someone else had tried to make me take the pills and he had always been very much against it.

'You should never ever take pills, Caroline – not if you don't know what they are.'

I wondered if he would mind if I went home now, for he no longer seemed to feel that I should take them, and I no longer felt I had to worry about hurting his feelings. But he still seemed to be waiting for something, and I still hated the way that he looked so cowed as he kept on staring at me, for it frightened me to feel that I could frighten an adult.

'Maybe I should take back the pills where I got them, and I'll get them to put on a nice, clean, new, label.' Now he only seemed to be chattering for the sake of it – saying anything that he hoped would please me.

'When I take back the bottle, Caroline – I'll complain to them about the label.'

'That's the best thing to do.'

All at once his manner changed, and he no longer seemed frightened, and the whites of his eyes seemed to turn mauve he looked so angry. 'If I take all the trouble to get you new pills – you've got to take them – and there's going to be no nonsense. People don't like you mucking around with them.'

Something in his new expression made me panic, for I saw that he had the same ruthlessly concentrated look on his face that I had seen so often whenever he put a horse at a jump, cracking it across its rump with his bone-handled crop, jabbing blood from its flanks with his spurs. A suspicion which had been burrowing like a blind, black mole through my brain ever since he had first showed me his pills, suddenly surfaced and turned from suspicion to certainty. McAfee was a poisoner . . . It all made sense to me now. If his pills were really pills to make you ride well – why had he insisted that I take them at night in this far-off wood? Why couldn't he have given them to me in the stables? I understood now why he had seemed so terrified that someone might see him giving them to me – why he had acted in such an odd, shifty way, rolling his eyes, and whispering, whenever he even mentioned them. I was now

123

quite certain that the word 'Poison' had once been written on the label, and he had scratched it off because he knew that I wouldn't take his pills if I read it.

I had only a confused idea why McAfee so wanted to poison me. But I was quite accustomed to finding many adult impulses inexplicable. And at that time the murderous plots of books and films were so interwoven in my mind with the threatening and violent images of various inner fears and fantasies, that I felt no particular need to find a good reason for McAfee's murderous intentions towards me. I found it explanation enough to assume that he must have always secretly hated me – all those years that he had been forced to take me riding through those endless Ulster lanes and gorse-fields. I wondered why I had never realised how serious he had always been when he had kept on telling me that he detested bad riders. For, finally, tonight he had tried to make me take poison, and I was quite certain that if I had been stupid enough to take his pills – by now I would have already been dead, and buried by him under some oak in this wood.

I made a dash, and I jumped on to my bicycle. McAfee appeared to be taken by surprise and quite unable to understand why I was suddenly crying.

'Caroline . . . Caroline . . . What have I done?' he kept repeating.

He made a gesture as though he was going to grab my back wheel, but then seemed to decide against it. I started peddling, and peddling, and I had the nightmarish feeling that my wheels were just churning, churning in the same mud rut. But when I turned to see if he was chasing me, I saw that he was standing quite still, looking very tiny, and dispirited, in the clearing. At my last sight of him, he was slowly loping on his stunted legs, like some lame animal down the bridle-path.

'Caroline . . . Caroline . . .' he shouted after me. 'Please . . . please . . . Never breathe a word!'

The only person that I ever told about my meeting with McAfee was Perdita. She agreed immediately that he was obviously a poisoner. We both felt that it would be very unsafe to tell this to anyone – for you could never tell what a man like that might do to you. We decided that we would never go riding with him again, and we would never go near the stables.

For many months McAfee went on sitting all day alone in the harness-room. He went on pointlessly polishing the bits of our unused bridles, soft-soaping our girths, rubbing yellow wax into our saddles. Our ponies grew fatter and fatter, from lack of exercise. McAfee went on curry-combing them, making them bran-mashes, plaiting up their manes with little red ribbons. Since Perdita and I seemed to have lost all interest in riding, it was decided after about a year that McAfee was a waste of money, and when he was fired our ponies were put out to grass.

When I see Perdita now we still often talk about McAfee, and our conversation always only turns into questions and finally becomes frustrating, and tiresome, like trying to do a crossword if you know that you will never see the answers. Always she asks me the same things. How did McAfee think that he could get away with it . . .? What were his pills, and how and where did he get hold of them . . .? How much did Mrs McAfee ever know . . .? How many other children were given similar pills by McAfee . . . ? If I had taken them what would . . .? 'Please . . . Please . . .' I always answer. 'I don't even want to talk about it. Please . . . Please . . . Could you just stop breathing a word!'

BETTY

In Ulster during the war I was looked after by a nurse-maid called Betty. She was plump, and flirtatious, and rather backward, and she told me that her mother was always praying for her because she didn't think that Betty had a hope of marrying, because no woman ever got married if they 'held themselves so cheap'. But Betty was always hopeful, and she squeezed some elderberries and she rubbed the juice on her freckles, and she went and had her ginger hair permed to a gollywog frizz in Bangor, and every day, clip clop, in her utility high-heeled shoes, she would take me walking past the hideous grey maze of Nissen huts of the American camp which squatted at the end of our drive.

'Say hello to the soldiers, Caroline. Ask them for some chewing-gum. It doesn't look funny for a child to do that.' And in the end Betty always got talking to the G.I.s and I remember one of them saying to her that he found there was so little to do with his leave in Ulster, that he would rather be sent to the front and lose a leg, than be stuck away in 'this god-forsaken fucking back of nowhere'.

'Don't you ever use such wicked language in front of a child! Can't you see she's listening? She listens to everything. She's very sly. She's never as deaf as she pretends to be. And I don't appreciate it very much myself. I don't think that's a nice thing to say to a girl about her country.' But I knew that Betty was only pretending to be angry, and that secretly she felt very much the same as him. She had told me that she prayed to God every night that the war would make it possible for her to end up as a G.I. bride.

'War's a terrible thing – but sometimes you have to be rather glad of it. At least it can give you a few opportunities. Kids and housework. Kids and more housework. That's all that any Ulsterman can offer you.'

Betty was always talking about the G.I. rations. 'You just take what one of those military fellows gets for lunch – and you give it to an Ulster family. They'd all be able to live on it until the baby was old enough to grow grey whiskers and pass on to a better world.'

Betty also never stopped talking to me about American salads. 'You just couldn't believe the salads that they have over there in the States. I've seen them in the magazines. They are all beautiful colours like the rainbow – they just make your mouth water. You could live all your life in Northern Ireland but you'd never get anything as colourful as that.'

'When I grow up I'm going to marry an American,' I told Betty.

'It's not up to you,' she said, 'it's up to God. And you better just pray that he'll be a bit good to you. You are not a bad wee girl when you are not in one of your sulks. And I must say that I wouldn't want to see you waste yourself on anything you'll ever find around here.'

The war never made what Betty wanted happen. Only one G.I. ever proposed to her. He gave her a tin of spam and two packets of American cigarettes as a present and he took her into Bangor and they played the pin-machines in the Fun Arcade. It was sunny that day and they walked along the seafront and then they sat on a bench. He told Betty that she looked as if she had trapped the sunshine in her hair, and she said that the way he talked made all the local fellows seem like speechless bullocks, and that you would never find an Ulsterman who used a shaving-lotion with that special delicious American smell. When they said goodbye he told her that he wanted to arrange for her to join him in Denver Colorado after the war was over.

The next time he took her out it was all a failure. When they went into Bangor, he tried to buy himself a soft-drink, but there was nowhere open because it was a Sunday. He then suddenly got in a terrible temper, and somehow he blamed Betty, and he started using insulting language about her country and said that he hadn't been able to find a place where you could go dancing for three months.

After that they went down on to the beach, for there was nothing else to do. All the Bangor streets were so dismal, and grey and deserted, that she felt that they might have both found it gayer to have taken a walk round a cemetery. The sky was very overcast that day and he never once said that she had trapped any sunshine in her hair. A lot of seagulls kept circling around overhead and he only spoke to complain that their screeching was getting on his nerves.

Once they got down on the beach, the sand was all pebbles and very un-comfortable, the seaweed had a strong sour smell of town sewage, and Betty said that the wind was coming in so hard from the channel that you thought that the Isle of Man would suddenly land in your lap. He got in an even fouler temper because they couldn't find any shelter and she felt that he was even blaming her for the wind.

While they were trailing around miserably by the sea-edge, to make things worse he suddenly got a pebble in his shoe, and she said that no child could have made more fuss about it, that he behaved as if he felt that his whole foot would have to be amputated. Betty tried to make a few jokes to cheer him up but he never laughed once, and when they finally sat down he used his army great-coat selfishly to cushion himself, never caring that the discomfort was far worse for Betty, for she was only wearing a thin little silky frock.

He kept staring sulkily out to sea and then he started muttering that he had 'just about had this fucking war'. And secretly Betty couldn't feel that he was really in the war, not when he was sitting there on the beach, on a Sunday, in Bangor.

He never stopped chain-smoking American cigarettes and he never offered her a single one. And then for no particular reason his mood changed and he started getting very fresh. But she said that it wasn't at all in a nice way – it had 'no respect'. Finally, somehow, there was some kind of a scuffle and something fell out of his pocket and she saw that it was a snap-shot of his wife and kids. 'Imagine going all the way to Denver Colorado, and finding that!'

Betty didn't mind too much because she knew that a whole new regiment of G.I.s was due to arrive from the States the following Saturday. 'There's plenty more where he comes from,' she said.

PIGGY

The damp, stone, Victorian passages smelt of football boots and antiseptic. The dining-room always had a lingering smell of bad stew. 'Madame Souri a un jardin,' droned on the French master, while outside the school the seagulls screeched as they circled through the mist that hung over Belfast Lough. Lessons were dreary, but they always seemed better than the breaks, when McDougal would get the boys to gang up on the new boys.

McDougal dominated Stoneyport Preparatory School partly by his character but mostly by his size. At eleven he was almost as tall as a full-grown man. He also had a thyroid condition which gave him additional power, as it made him freakishly overweight. He was a gingery-haired near-albino, with a snout-like nose which had given him the nickname of Piggy. He had powdery white eyelashes, and his tiny eyes were pale, and weak, and twitching. He had eyes which always seemed to be excited by some new and unpleasant plan.

McDougal could always get all the other boys to carry out his wishes, and the way they obeyed him was abject, and lacked any affection. No one in the school liked Piggy McDougal, but they all respected and feared him, because he had hatreds which were formed, while theirs were still diffused and shifting. McDougal's hatreds were so unswerving, and dependable, and had such a simplicity, that like an efficient transport service introduced by force on a country verging on chaos, they were welcomed by all the boys who felt themselves imperilled by their own state of confused pre-adolescent anarchy.

McDougal hated two things, new boys and Catholics. If he could have found a new boy who was also a Catholic . . . But that was impossible at Stoneyport Preparatory School for no Catholic had ever been admitted there. The headmaster had no wish for the school to be burned down. In Ulster things got around very fast — people felt very strongly — you couldn't be too careful.

McDougal was therefore cheated of a chance to confront his supreme arch-enemy. But every term brought him a new little troupe of new boys. He had also discovered that there was a derelict cottage just ouside the school grounds in which there lived a whole family of Catholics.

I

Even now I still wonder how McDougal found out that the cottage was full of Catholics. Did his obsession make him more than usually sensitive to all the suspicions and rumours which were always trickling along the Ulster grapevine? Or did McDougal simply make a mistake? Was that family never really Catholic at all? Did McDougal suspect this when he organised us on half-holidays, and fired us all on so that the whole school would go out to stone them? Did he think that this family looked so dilapidated and depressed — that this family looked so hunted when the stones came showering down on them from behind the hedges — that they looked so exactly like Catholics they deserved whatever they had coming to them?

'Blackwood,' McDougal said to me one day, 'I don't like girls being allowed in this school. It makes the whole place look feeble.'

I was only allowed to go to Stoneyport Preparatory School for Boys as a favour because it was wartime, and with petrol rationing it was the only private school which was anywhere near our house. I was a day-girl while all the boys were boarders. I arrived every morning in a pony and trap.

Ever since my first day at Stoneyport I had been plagued by the terrible fear that McDougal would eventually turn on me. I knew only too well how much he disliked anything which he felt was odd. He detested Derry Green because he had a birth-mark. He disliked all the boys who wore spectacles, and gold bands on their teeth. He always tormented the ones who wore plain grey socks instead of the proper Stoneyport uniform kind, which were grey with a thin rim of blue round their tops. McDougal's obsessive hatred of new boys was mainly caused by the fact that their fluster, their general look of lostness, and their homesick 'blubbing', made him find them all extremely odd.

McDougal would stand on the cricket field, and his thyroid-condition thighs always looked inappropriate, they were so much too massive for his shorts. McDougal nearly always seemed to be accompanied by Johnson, and McAlister, Barcley minor, and McBane. He dwarfed them by his height and his bulk, but they were active and they were wiry. The four of them often appeared to be like the gun-dogs which snarl around a gamekeeper's boot. McDougal could invariably assemble them the very second that he needed them. It was as if he owned some kind of dog-whistle to which they were sensitive though its timbre was too high for the average human ear.

'Get that sneak!' McDougal would shout. They were so well-trained, they would get the new boy down on his back in a second. They dragged him to a grassy patch behind a great clump of gorse bushes where no master would be able to hear any screams. Johnson and McAlister would twist his wrists and pinion them behind his head. Barcley minor and McBane would sit on his feet. 'Now he's going to start blubbing. The bloody, feeble, little blubber!' Then a crowd would form as it does with a street accident.

'Someone hold his nose!' McDougal would shout. Some boy always volunteered. McDougal would step forward like a general taking a salute. He would open the flies of his shorts with the ritualistic slowness of a churchman divesting himself of his robes. His penis always looked very pink and swollen as he held it like a pistol and took his careful aim. 'Hold his nose tight. Make him open his mouth. Bloody little fool! The bloody little blubber!'

The new boy would be writhing frantically on the grass, scarlet, and scratched, and choking. The golden jet of McDougal's urine would sometimes miss his mouth, splash on to his hair, or his spectacles, trickle down over his tear-stained cheeks. 'Keep him still damn you!'

Sometimes McDougal's aim was very good. 'Keep on holding his nose. I want him to swallow it!' When he had finished McDougal always smiled with a fatuous conceit. 'I think he swallowed quite a bit. Who else wants a turn?' The members of the crowd would file up, boy after boy, and they would all open up their flies. There would be the same struggling, and choking, and screams, the same near misses, the same good aims. Finally, McDougal would tire of watching performances which he clearly felt were very feeble copies of his own. 'Let him go. He must have drunk enough pee to make him stink like a lavatory.' 'Is it poisonous to drink so much?' I once heard a nervous weasel-like boy ask McDougal. He shrugged irritably as he answered. 'Who the Hell cares?'

When McDougal told me that he didn't like girls being allowed in the school, I knew that exactly what I had always feared – that my oddness would make me one of his special targets – was just about to happen. Previously I had always managed to keep in with McDougal. At that time I felt that the most vital thing in my whole life was keeping in with McDougal. Far more slyly craven than any of the boys, I had always treated him with a consistent and repulsive sycophancy. I would laugh at all his jokes, which were invariably cruel, but rarely funny. I gave him my sweet-ration coupons, and stole cigarettes from home and brought them to him. 'Blackwood's not bad for a girl,' he would sometimes say, looking at me with tiny, white-lashed eyes.

My abject slavishness was not the only reason why McDougal had never set his hound-dogs on to me. McDougal had once told me that he had never seen a girl without any clothes on. He then kept dropping more and more

131

threatening hints. And finally he asked me if I would agree to undress in front of him. Far too intimidated to risk getting myself into his special bad favour, I agreed. McDougal then decided the undressing should be done in some rhododendron bushes which were safely far from the school. As we set off together, I found, inevitably, that he had ordered Johnson, and McAlister, Barcley minor, and McBane, to come tagging along too.

All four of them were desperately shy and awkward. As they walked beside me up to the bushes, they were as downcast as mutes escorting a coffin. They stood in a semi-circle in a hollow walled by rhododendrons. There was a respectful hush as I undressed and the whole occasion seemed more and more like a burial.

No one seemed to get the slightest excitement or pleasure from my strip-tease. I felt mortified and humiliated, and the boys appeared to feel mortified and humiliated too. The very leaves of the surrounding rhododendrons seemed to be drooping, as if they too were distressed by a feeling of anti-climax, squalor, and shame.

In Ulster at that time it was quite common to view nakedness as something to be feared, like murder, and Johnson and McAlister, Barcley minor and McBane, looked really frightened. They might as well have been standing outside the Headmaster's study waiting to be caned. And to my surprise, for I had such an exaggerated inner picture of his omnipotence, it was McDougal who was obviously the most petrified of all. Standing there in the hollow, he lost all his confidence, he lost all his authority. We all had an in-built Presbyterian prudery, but McDougal seemed to feel more pressured by it than any of us. The nervous blink of his white eyelashes became far worse than usual. His mouth was slack and trembly. He kept fidgeting with his hands.

'I've never seen a girl before.' He whispered this with a kind of horror, and he sounded almost tearful. 'I didn't know it would be like this.'

By increasing everyone else's embarrassment, McDougal appeared to be increasing his own. He seemed to know he was doing this and yet be unable to stop himself. 'I'm an only child,' he suddenly mumbled, as if he felt this explained something very important. He was prolonging an occasion which was becoming more and more painful by the minute, for he seemed unable to decide how long he ought to go on looking. The presence of the other boys pinioned him. In front of them he was ashamed not to get his money's worth. He didn't dare do what he so clearly wanted to, put a stop to the whole thing and get away.

'Have you had the curse yet?' McDougal's porcine face, usually so florid, was ashen, and his forehead was streaked with nervous mottles. Instinctively I sensed that I must not tell him that I had never had it. I could tell by the superstitious terror that I saw in his tiny eyes, that the curse was anathema to him, that anyone who had had it could use it as a weapon to terrorise him.

When I refused to answer, my silence seemed to chill him, for I noticed that his teeth were chattering like those of a winter swimmer. All at once, heady with the realisation that for once the roles were reversed, that McDougal's fear of me was now far greater than my longstanding fear of him, I put on all my clothes without caring whether he wanted me to keep them off, and I started walking back to the school, knowing he wouldn't dare to make a move to force me back into the bushes. I sensed with an immense and spiteful pleasure that he had temporarily lost all control of the other boys — that they felt he had failed them in a situation when they had looked to him for leadership — that they had noticed that his behaviour throughout the undressing had been exactly what he had taught them to despise. McDougal had been 'feeble'. His whole comportment had been odd. And most disillusioning of all, throughout the whole dismal occasion McDougal had looked as if he was just about to 'blub'.

All the rest of that term McDougal appeared to retain his peculiar fear of me. He stopped asking me to steal him sweets and cigarettes. He never made the boys gang up on me. He never spoke a single word to me. He hardly seemed to see me. During lessons he took great care never to choose a desk which was anywhere near the one where I sat. And all the time I knew that McDougal was very aware of me, that he was deliberately avoiding me as if he felt that I had the evil eye.

I was only too glad to have this inglorious power over him, only too relieved to have temporary immunity from his attacks, but I never lost the nagging feeling that there was little hope that this happy state of things would last.

When one day McDougal suddenly told me that he didn't like girls being allowed in the school, his face had such a look of loathing that I realised that all those quiet months his resentment and his belligerence had only been storing up for this moment.

'If you don't want to have your life made Hell for you in this school, Blackwood — you are going to have to make yourself useful.'

McDougal then told me that he wanted to arrange a raid after school — that he wanted to have another bash at the Catholic fuckers who lived in the cottage near the village of Ballycraig. He said he wanted me to collect his ammunition and be his ammunition-bearer. 'If you don't want to get a stone in your mouth, Blackwood – you better see that I don't have a moment when I don't have something in my hand.'

After school McDougal started his raid. Johnson and McAlister, Barcley minor and McBane, walked in front with him like generals. I followed immediately behind them dragging a load of stones in a pillow-slip, and the rest of the school came after me in a straggling file.

As we marched we all had a feeling of excitement and release. It was a Wednesday, and a half-holiday. Usually everyone dreaded the dullness of half-holidays when they would lounge around, home-sick, write letters to their parents asking them for stamps, or just lie on their stomachs in the school fields and restlessly suck the juice out of the stalks of pieces of grass.

But on the way up to the cottage, the jail-sentenced mood that half-holidays usually brought to Stoneyport pupils seemed to have suddenly blown away like thistle seed. 'They can't expel all of us,' someone said as we passed out of bounds. 'They must have noticed we've all gone. I bet they know what we are doing, and I bet they don't really mind.' Our usual fear and hatred of all the masters had suddenly vanished. We felt that we had their unspoken approval – that their power was behind us. We had lost all memory of the torture of all our daily gangings-up, splittings-up, suckings-up.

For one moment on our march we all felt that we were rather a marvellous little unit. Everyone was elated, even the new boys, feeling that we would all stand by each other, feeling that the cottage was malignly advancing on us, rather than the reverse, feeling that in view of the threatening provocation from the cottage we were all extremely brave.

The cottage lay in an isolated position about half a mile from the village of Ballycraig. It was a dirt-streaked, whitewashed little building, and it was roofed with a moth-eaten thatch over which tarpaulins had been roped in its weakest patches to keep out the rain.

McDougal ordered all the boys to surround it, to station themselves behind the safe cover of trees and hedges, to see that none of the occupants managed to escape. Then, bulky and thyroid, he walked out into the open, and he started the attack. He bombarded the cottage with stones which I handed him from my pillow-slip. His aim was very bad and it took a long time before any of them hit the tiny dark windows. But eventually this happened and an old woman came out into the garden in which there grew a few rows of bluish cabbages, amongst which pecked a small coterie of under-fed hens.

At first she just stood there looking puzzled. She had untidy white hair, and was wearing a drooping long black skirt and an apron. Her arms were

134

red and chapped, she had a collapsed mouth, and her skin was a criss-cross of deep wrinkles.

'Fire!' McDougal shouted, and all the boys hurled their stones at her. The chickens all squawked, a sheep-dog started to bark, and she gave a scream and ran back into the cottage. There was a sound of commotion inside it, and shadowy faces came peering through the tiny windows.

Her husband finally came out. He was wearing an old tweed cap and overalls, and he was as white-haired and tissued with wrinkles as she was. 'Fire!' shouted McDougal, and the old man retreated back into the cottage.

McDougal was just about to order his troops to advance on the cottage when suddenly out came five of the old woman's grandsons. They were all teenagers and the oldest must have been about nineteen. They wore open shirts, and heavy farming boots, and one of them was carrying a pitchfork. As though they had one voice between them, they all started cursing, and they picked up any stick or stone that was to be found on the ground and started hurling them at their hidden enemies who were crouching behind the hedges.

Seeing the size of the grandsons, hearing the ferocious cursing of the grandsons, seeing that the grandsons were starting to throw pieces of iron farming-equipment, and big rocks and heavy logs, the Stoneyporters instantly lost their solidarity. Like a flock of migrating birds they all left their strategic positions and ran back up a hill to where they could watch the rest of the battle from the safety of some dense trees. Far more frightened of the grandsons than I was of McDougal, I dumped down the pillowslip of stones beside him, and followed the deserters.

Abandoned by everyone, even by Johnson, McAlister, Barcley minor and McBane, McDougal stood alone in the open in front of the cottage. He seemed to lack the initiative even to take cover. He just went on ineptly standing there. His behaviour was much the same as it had been during the undressing. It was as if his own cowardice were giving him courage by making him too frightened to move.

McDougal kept on picking stones out of the pillow-slip, and he went on throwing them in a weak and mechanical way at the cottage. His gestures no longer appeared to be aggressive, they were clearly so mindless and unplanned.

Usually McDougal looked massive and formidable, but now it was as if his very bulk, like his bravado, had suddenly diminished. A pink-faced, flabby David, for once he had a certain pathos standing there alone confronting the five grandson Goliaths.

If the grandsons had realised that all their hidden Stoneyport enemies had long ago done their rat-scuttle from behind the hedges, they might have killed McDougal. Not grasping this, they were still cautious, and instead of advancing on him they stayed in crafty positions keeping behind the cover of some chicken-sheds.

They had found an ammunition treasure-trove of horse-shoes, and as they kept hurling them at McDougal it was only the iron-weight of these objects which prevented a lot of them from striking him. But eventually one of the youths did a super-throw, and McDougal gave a howl, and suddenly he was hopping on one leg and clutching at his other knee. The pain in his leg apparently returned some sense of self-preservation to him, and he retreated limping behind a hedge, and the grandsons booed and cheered.

It was all over. And then suddenly a six-year-old girl, wearing a grimy little crumpled frock and carrying a school satchel, came down the lane which led to the cottage. Unaware that there had just been a battle at her home, she was whistling and skipping as she came. Her jauntiness, in his state of humiliation and defeat, obviously enraged McDougal. He picked up one last stone and threw it from behind his hedge with what remained of his strength, and it hit her smash in the face.

She fell down in the lane and her face was spurting blood and there was a thundering rumble of anger from the grandsons and they all came rushing out from behind the chicken-sheds waving pitch-forks, spades, and scythes. McDougal and all the rest of us who had been watching from the hill were seized by a collective panic and we all started running back towards the school. It was as if we were trying to run away, not only from the pitch-forks of the grandsons, but also from the guilt of the hideous thing we now felt we all had done.

'Do you think they will ring up the police?' I heard McBane ask McDougal once we were back at the school and sitting around on desks in an empty classroom.

'Those kind of people don't have telephones,' McDougal said. On the surface he was calm but the nervous blink of his eyelashes showed his agitation. 'Do you think she was blinded?' McBane asked him. I expected McDougal to give some kind of shrugging, contemptuous answer. But McDougal didn't say anything.

His silence apparently infuriated McBane and it was the only time I ever saw him turn on McDougal. 'You bloody fool!' he said, 'we are all in for trouble. And it was you who got us into it.'

'What are you making the big fuss about?' McDougal's tone was plaintive.

136

'Nothing's going to happen. I bet you that nothing is going to happen.' McDougal was right, for nothing ever did happen, but McBane refused to believe him.

'There's going to be bloody ructions,' McBane kept on grumbling.

'Those kind of people don't go to the police,' McDougal said. 'Those kind of people don't know how to. I just bet you that nothing ever happens.'

'You bloody fool!' McBane said. He jabbed the point of a compass into a desk as if he was trying to run it through the bulky body of McDougal.

MEMORIES OF ULSTER*

> And for all that I found there I might as well be
> Where the Mountains of Mourne sweep down to the sea.

Many people from Ulster have always felt that the man who wrote that song was a liar. 'If the fellow once managed to get himself out of Northern Ireland,' a woman from Belfast once said to me, 'it's a bit hard to believe he's all that sincere when he pretends he was always fretting to get back. But the tune's all right, and the sentiment is all right. And in Ulster, of course,' she added, 'the tune and the sentiment have always been the thing.'

That was long ago. But I still feel surprised whenever I hear Ulster mentioned in the news. It always used to seem like the archetypal place where nothing would, or could, ever happen. For as long as I can remember, boredom has seemed to be hanging over Northern Ireland like the grey mists that linger over her loughs. Boredom has seemed to be sweating out of the blackened Victorian buildings of Belfast, running down every tram-line of her dismal streets. Now, when Northern Ireland is mentioned, the word 'internment' rattles through every sentence like the shots of a repeating rifle. And yet for years and years so many Ulster people, both Catholic and Protestant, have felt that they were 'interned' in Ulster – interned by the gloom of her industrialised provinciality, by her backwaterishness, her bigotry and her tedium.

In 1940, war was seen as a solution. 'All the American troops will liven things up a bit round here.' But the last war never broke the back of Ulster's boredom. Everyone kept predicting – almost with pleasure – that the Belfast docks would be a prime German target, that Hitler would almost certainly launch his invasion via Northern Ireland. All the signposts were swivelled round in the Ulster lanes to trick his troops, and force tanks which had hoped to roll towards Ballynahinch into ending up in Ballygalley. However effective all these crafty precautions would have been in the event of a full-scale Axis landing, they turned out to be needless. There were very few raids, and one of these by error bombed what Protestant Northerners called 'collaborationist' Dublin. This was said to be an act of God.

*Written in 1972.

138

The American troops livened things up very little in Ulster. They hadn't much to do except hand out chewing-gum to the kids. They slouched miserably through their 'duration' – and then they were gone. The few bonneted black faces which appeared in Ulster prams were the only memorable trace that they left of their unenjoyable stay.

And day after day – post-war, just as they had pre-war – in the grey squares of the Ulster villages groups of men in tweed caps, most of them toothless and out of work, went on standing around in huddles. They would rub their hands and mutter, and sometimes have a smoke, like people on a platform waiting endlessly for some cancelled train. And day after day – post-war, just as they had pre-war – in the wealthy suburbs of Belfast the wives of industrialists went on reading the Bible, drinking their sherry and eating scones. In those days all their houses were meant to contain that most curious of rooms known as 'the parlour'. The parlour was always musty and unused. There every stick of silver, every horse-show trophy and spoon, every candelabra and christening-cup, that the family had ever acquired was always laid out day and night, as though in defiant display of the rewards of Protestant virtue. Far too valuable to be used, and very heavily insured, there used to be a desolation to all this silver, which was polished daily by the maid and seemed to be perpetually waiting on its mahogany table as if in preparation for some longed-for, but never-arriving occasion. And very much the same effect used to be created, in the rooms which were in use for entertaining, by all the plaster Peter Scott geese, which were nailed so that they appeared to be flying past the photograph of the Royal Family in a freedom arc up the side of the wall. Sometimes one had the feeling that these status-symbol geese themselves secretly knew that their flight was an illusion: that they were just as static as their owners, that they would never fly out of these stifling, expensive interiors, where the light could hardly penetrate all the Gothic-cathedral stained-glass of the windows.

Then there were the Ulster Sundays. Post-war, there were still the Ulster Sundays: the war changed them not at all. On Sundays all the towns were still closed down, so that they seemed like the ghost towns of Colorado, and the Day of Rest went on being so well-observed that the serving of a cup of tea was still damned as a violation. When anyone died, people still went on saying that they feared it was a 'judgment': that the dead one must have gone out driving, or drunk a Guinness, or read some novel on a Sunday.

And the war never changed the sermons which were preached on those Ulster Sundays, and the families still trailed off to listen to them. They would

139

go all dressed up with hats and gloves and coins for the collection, taking their bored and dressed-up children. One particular sermon I heard in Ulster has always stayed with me. It was delivered on a Christmas Day, and the minister preached it from a pulpit decorated with holly. He said that on this special day he would like to start by quoting 'the most beautiful words in the English language'. His choice was curious : 'The womb of a virgin hath he not abhorred.' In his own terms, it was a daring choice. And some puritanical hesitation seemed to panic him, forcing him into a slip. He paused dramatically before delivering his words, and then boomed them out in ringing church-chant tones : 'The worm of a virgin hath he not abhorred.' I looked round his congregation. Surely they would have some reaction to this most unusual Christmas Day text. But all the scrubbed faces seemed to be in their usual trance. Glazed eyes just went on staring despondently at dusty hassocks, at the bleakness of the altar, stripped of all ornamentation to make a contrast with the idolatrous churches of the Papacy. Not one single person reacted to the minister's beautiful words – for not one person had heard them. His congregation had been interned by his sermons for far too long for his words to have any more power to penetrate the defensive depths of their devout deafness.

'Do you come from Northern Ireland?' I remember Foxy Falk barking the question at me years ago at an Oxford dinner. I was used to contemptuous responses from English people whenever I answered this question. 'The South of Ireland is very nice,' was all they would usually say. Or else, making one feel like some kind of mongrel impostor : 'Oh, then you are not even proper Irish at all.' But I felt that the question, when asked by Foxy Falk, was going to lead to something a little different. A collector of Ming vases, Cézannes and Persian carpets, he was a man who said that he believed in 'the rule of the élite and the artist'. He was tyrannical, reading Keats's letters aloud to people who had little desire to hear them, forbidding anyone in his household to use the telephone because he felt that it had ruined the art of conversation – and thereby creating daily difficulties as to grocery orders etc. He would intimidate by his spluttering rages, which made one fear that the boil of his anger would crack his arteries. He was famous for the fact that he had once been Pavlova's lover.

'Do you come from Ulster?' I saw that the charge behind his question had already turned his whole face to a tomato-coloured balloon. Then his fist came smashing down on to the table so that the knives went shivering against the glasses. 'All I can say is that the place where you come from ought to be blown up! It ought to be blown skyhigh, and wiped from the face of this earth!' If he felt like that . . . I found myself staring blankly at his poor old turkey wattles, which were wobbling with agitation as they dripped down over his high Edwardian collar.

Then he calmed a little and explained that Pavlova at the height of her fame had danced in Belfast, and that the theatre had been totally empty except for two people. He claimed that she had never felt so insulted and distressed in her whole life – that Belfast was the only place in the world which had ever given her such a criminal reception.

Maybe because of the bombastic way the whole subject had been approached, and because I felt I was being personally blamed for the disastrous unsuccess of her visit, all I could feel was a sudden impatience with both Pavlova and her lover. Why were they so astounded by what to me seemed to be so very unastounding? What could have made them think that her dance could ever set the grimy dockyards of Belfast dancing? When had that most austere of cities ever pretended for one moment that its prime interest was the dance?

I thought of the Ulster Protestants. Surely they had enough problems without having to be 'wiped from the face of this earth' for being a poor audience. A fear of Catholics bred into them from childhood until it became instinctive like a terror of spiders. Their lifelong drill of eccentric Ulster commandments. 'Never drink from the same glass that a Catholic has drunk from. Any such glass should be broken immediately.' And then their feeling of always being beleaguered, with the enemy pressing its full weight against the feeble ribbon of the border. Their suspicion that the enemy's prohibition on birth-control was a crafty long-term plan to out-breed them. Finally, their way of seeing the enemy – it's a very common way of seeing enemies – as dirty, lazy and cruel, plotting and promiscuous, and with one extra unforgivable vice – prone to dancing on a Sunday.

What happened? Everyone asks this as they look at the rubbled streets of Belfast and Londonderry on the television. The question never seems to be well answered, and only leads to more questions. If there had been no Catholics, would the Ulster Protestants have found it necessary to invent them? Certainly for years and years they provided the only spark of thrill and threat which could blast the monotony of the Ulster everyday. Month after month I remember listening to the same repeating rumours that the Catholics were marching up from Dublin – 'mustering' on the border – and infiltrating industry. Did all those interminable Ulster sermons seem less tedious when it was envisaged that iron-handed Papists might very soon try to put a stop to them? Did the polluted belch of Northern industry seem less hideous if it was felt that greedy Papal fingers were tentacling out to grasp the factories?

Can there be a boredom so powerful that it finally acts like an explosive? Marx said that the cottage must never be too near the castle. If England was the castle, was the provincial cottage of Ulster just a little bit too near?

'Wouldn't you think that people might be less bigoted in this day and age?' English people keep on asking me that. 'You certainly would think so,' I answer. And immediately I find myself doing a double-take. 'Why would you think that they might be?' I wonder. 'What reasons are there for thinking so?'

Every day the Ulster victims are flashed on the British television screens. They stutter out their tragedies in accents so unintelligible to the English that they might as well be speaking Swahili, and then they are cut off in mid-sentence for lack of television time.

When the Reverend Ian Paisley makes an occasional BBC appearance he seems awkward, oafish and provincial. He seems to lose all his rhetorical teeth when he is speaking to an English audience. He needs the roll and rattle of the Orange kettledrums to accompany his impassioned and oracular calls to duty. He needs to have his fanatical congregation, and King Billy of the Boyne, and The Lord, behind him. To see him on the BBC, who could believe that he could be idolised in Ulster? Who would ever think that he was an innovator — that back home in his Northern Irish church he has invented something quite as new as the 'paper collection'? For Ian Paisley has said that the Lord wants no more coins . . . During his services, when the collection plate is passed round the congregation, the pounds pile up on it like great mounds of crumpled Kleenexes. But then when the plate is handed in to him, Dr Paisley refuses to bless it. He just looks at it in sad silence and he shakes his enormous head. 'The Lord,' he says, 'is not going to be very pleased with this.' And the plate is sent back to the congregation for another round.

And while the Reverend's collection plate is circulating, the IRA seem less and less heroic as they blow the legs and arms off typists, and plant their gelignite wires across the routes of the school buses. And yet Ulster's rate of mental disease keeps on dropping as the troubles persist. Doctors claim they have never known it so low. All the while the Ulster Defence Association, dressed up like Ku Klux Klansmen, like Knights Templar from Outer Space, are drilling, and recruiting from the Orange Lodges of Scotland. They too set up their 'no go' areas and their kangaroo courts. Last week I spoke to a Protestant who lives in County Down. 'You don't like to go out at night,' she said.

'You feel that you might run into some roaming regiment of UDA with all their guns, and their goggles, and fish-net stockings over their mouths. And you feel that they might not like the look of you. They might set up a kangaroo court, and you'd be tried in their pouch.' War games . . . And on both sides how many really want them to end one can sometimes despondently wonder. Has the whole province become intoxicated with its new-found power to seize the international headlines from its ancient overshadowing and world-important sister, England? Does it now feel some perverse and destructive terror of sinking back into a humdrum and peaceful obscurity in which the individual Ulsterman will no longer feel the superiority and glory of springing from a world-famed trouble-spot?

'Why not move all the Protestants out?' English liberals keep suggesting. 'Why not move all the Catholics out?' Another common, and less liberal, suggestion. Both suggestions make it all sound so easy, like moving pinned flags on a staff map. Families, farms, occupations, the tie to the place of birth — all these things are made to seem like trifling, selfish quirks, which should be sacrificed for the greater good of the community. But who is going to decide which community most deserves this greater good? Then you are back again with an 'Ulster problem'.

'Why can't they all just get on with one another?' The English can seem very smug at the moment . . . If the IRA started hurling high explosives into the shopping-centres of Maidstone or Colchester, how long would it take before Catholic families living in the areas began to feel afraid of reprisals?